The Social Brain

Other Books by Michael S. Gazzaniga

THE BISECTED BRAIN (1970)

FUNDAMENTALS OF PSYCHOLOGY (1973)

THE INTEGRATED MIND, with Joseph LeDoux (1978)

PSYCHOLOGY (1980)

FUNDAMENTALS OF NEUROSCIENCE,
with Bruce T. Volpe and Diana Steen (1980)

THE SOCIAL BRAIN

Discovering the Networks of the Mind

MICHAEL S. GAZZANIGA

Basic Books, Inc., Publishers New York

Library of Congress Cataloging-in-Publication Data

Gazzaniga, Michael S.
The social brain.

Includes index.
1. Brain—Localization of functions. 2. Split brain. 3. Belief and doubt. 4. Neuropsychology. I. Title. [DNLM: 1. Brain—physiology—popular works. 2. Neuropsychology—popular works. 3. Social Values—popular works. WL 103 G289s]
QP385.G394 1985 612'.825 85–47563
ISBN 0–465–07850–8

Printed in the United States of America
Designed by Vincent Torre
86 87 88 HC 9 8 7 6 5 4 3 2

To the memory of Jeffrey David Holtzman

Scientist, Friend, Companion

CONTENTS

PREFACE

THIS IS A STORY about a scientific discovery, about its evolution and ultimately its effect on my personal understanding of social process.

Looking back over the last twenty-five years, I see how little we can foretell our future. From personal habits to scientific pursuits, our year-to-year endeavors change in ways that are totally unpredictable. What do not change are initial unanswered questions and, for me, those centered on how brain science might address problems of personal consciousness and through those a wider understanding of social processes. Some highly intelligent people can marvel over the elucidation of a phenomenon and are quite happy to leave it hanging in a factual capsule. Others are plagued with the secondary question of how a fact relates to a value, or to a personal understanding of life. While most scientific facts do not directly relate to broader social realities, some do. I think I have come across such connections, which is one reason for my writing this book.

In this book I recount how my experience in brain and psychological research has led to a mechanistic understanding of the way our brains are organized to generate our cognitions and, ultimately, our beliefs. Personal beliefs are what we are all about. We live and die by our commitments to particular views of life. What is it about the human brain that finds the formation of beliefs so central to its operation? Is there an identifiable logic to human brain organization that predicts which phenomena relate to belief formation? I address these and many other questions, but only after what I hope is an enlightening and even entertaining account of my brain research activities over the last twenty-five years.

I tell the story chronologically, as it happened. My first draft, however, was not written that way. There I fell into the usual scientific posture of describing and explaining an idea formally, in an order that implied that the theoretical construction argued was preformed in the mind, that substantiating experiments were carried out, and the results were presented to the world as an inexorable product of cold logic. Of course, precious few pieces of human knowledge ever emerge in that way, although most descriptions of scientific odysseys lead the reader to believe that research always progresses logically.

The story is now presented in three parts. First I relate how my understanding of the basic principles of brain organization, as learned from studying unique populations of neurologically impaired patients, argues for a particular view of brain function that I call the modular view. The data suggest that our mental lives amount to a reconstruction of the independent activities of the many brain systems we all possess. A confederation of mental systems resides within us. Metaphorically, we humans are more of a sociological entity than a single unified psychological entity. We have a social brain.

I then consider the implications of these ideas from the perspective of archaeology as well as from an interpretation of historical records related to the formation of religious beliefs. (It will become obvious later why I make these connections.) And finally, in the last chapter, I argue that my basic findings in brain research lead to a particular view of culture. It is not a chapter for the timid. Understanding human biologic and psychologic relations is still a most primitive enterprise. As our understanding of these processes deepens, so too will our understanding of social process. Yet, what I hope this chapter will suggest is that the ultimate and proper task of scientists is to work on these problems in an attempt to achieve such a synthesis.

Preface

I am accustomed to writing in a scientific style that requires references for everything. The wrath of one's colleagues when they think their ideas are not properly cited can scarcely be imagined. Since, however, this book is as much a personal narrative as a scientific study, I have compromised by providing source notes only for direct quotes and other specific references.

Thanks are due to the many people and institutions who helped me carry out this exercise.

I am most indebted to Jeffrey Holtzman, to whom this book is dedicated. He encouraged me and humored me throughout my work. His criticisms were unrelenting but always constructive. His tragic death from Wegener's disease in the spring of 1985 has created an emptiness in my life that will not soon be filled. He was the stuff of science, of life. He was unique.

I am indebted to Stephen Kosslyn, Nisson Schechter, Ira Black, and Michael Posner for their close readings of an early version of the manuscript, and for their many helpful suggestions. Thanks also go to Edgar Zurif, Gary Lynch, Ofer Bar-Yosef, and Robert Sommerville for their criticisms. I am also indebted to many of the principals in my intellectual life, including Leon Festinger, David Premack, and George Miller. All gave help and suggestions. At a practical level, my secretary, Christine Black, worked tirelessly as she always does, and Kitty Miller made a valiant effort to turn my prose into English. Most important, I thank all of the wonderful patients who made this work possible.

General support came from the Sloan Foundation, the McKnight Foundation, and the U.S. Public Health Service. I was able to write this particular book as the result of a generous fellowship from the John Solomon Guggenheim Memorial Foundation. Finally, my profound thanks to the staff at Basic Books, and especially to Jo Ann Miller, my editor. She made it all work.

The Social Brain

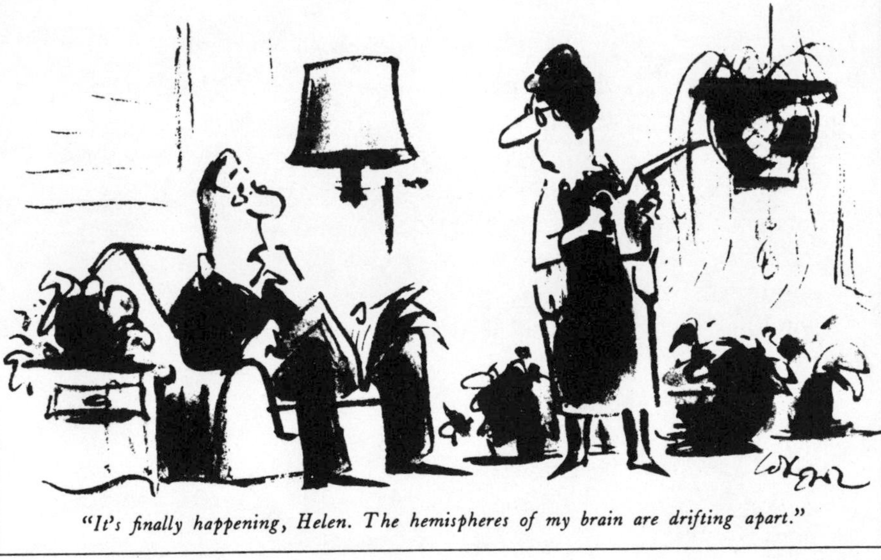

"It's finally happening, Helen. The hemispheres of my brain are drifting apart."

CHAPTER 1

The Interpretive Brain

BELIEVING is what we humans do best—we may believe that there is a God, or that the ACLU does or does not do good work—and we are in fact the only species to do so. What is there about the human brain or mind that endows us with this unique capacity? And, more important, in what ways does this remarkable ability relate to how we create and order the world around us? In this book I propose to demonstrate a new and vital link between the way our brains are organized and the way we construct beliefs—a link that I hope will help us gain a greater understanding of human culture in general and of the important connection between biological processes and critical issues in human behavior.

Beliefs stand at the end point of much of our cognitive activity. They are measurable properties of our mental life and they are, needless to say, powerful in determining much of what we accept as true about the world. Beliefs are central to the human experience, yet until recently the topic of how beliefs are formed and why we are so committed to them has been a topic more for philosophers and novelists than for laboratory scientists.

However, recent advances in our understanding of how the brain and mind are organized are changing this view. In fact, right now we humans have more insight into why we behave the way we do than we have ever had before. And it is this knowledge, gained in large part from the careful study of neurologically disordered patients, that opens the door to a new understanding of the fixed characteristics of our species.

We begin by taking a new view of the organization of the brain itself. Many prevalent theories about human thought have argued that problem solving occurs only at the level of conscious experience and that it is the product of the human language system per se. It has been a major assumption of many investigators in psychological research that the elements of our thought processes proceed serially in our "consciousness" for construction into cognitions. I think this notion of linear, unified conscious experience is dead wrong.

In contrast, I argue that the human brain has a modular-type organization. By modularity I mean that the brain is organized into relatively independent functioning units that work in parallel. The mind is not an indivisible whole, operating in a single way to solve all problems. Rather, there are many specific and identifiably different units of the mind dealing with all the information they are exposed to. The vast and rich information impinging on our brains is broken up into parts, and many systems start at once to work on it. These modular activities frequently operate apart from our conscious verbal selves. That does not mean they are "unconscious" or "preconscious" processes and outside our capacity to isolate and understand them. Rather, they are processes going on in parallel to our conscious thought, and contributing to our conscious structure in identifiable ways. At the level of conscious experience, we frequently ask ourselves where particular ideas came from when they appear in our consciousness. For example, when we write, we suddenly think of the exact way to phrase an idea. Where does such an insight come from? We don't seem to know. We seem only to have access to the product of these brain modules and not to the process itself.

These relatively independent modular units can actually discharge and produce real behaviors. With regular frequency we find ourselves engaged in activities that seem to come out of nowhere. Everything from eating atypical foods to forming uncommon relationships occurs, and at one level these activities appear to start up from scratch. Through experiments to be reported in this book, we are beginning to learn how this occurrence comes about at a mechanistic level.

The realization that the mind has a modular organization suggests that some of our behavior should be accepted as capricious and that a particular behavior might have no origins in our conscious thought process. For example, we just happen to eat frogs' legs for the first time or we decide to read a different kind of book. But as we shall see, we humans resist the interpretation that such behaviors are capricious because we seem to be endowed with an endless capacity to generate hypotheses as to why we engage in any behavior.

In short, our species has a special brain component I will call the "interpreter." Even though a behavior produced by one of these modules can be expressed at any time during our waking hours, this special interpreter accommodates and instantly constructs a theory to explain why the behavior occurred. While the interpreter does not actually know why there was an impulse to consume frogs' leg it might hypothesize, "Because I want to learn about French food." This special capacity, which is a brain component found in the left dominant hemisphere of right-handed humans, reveals how important the carrying out of behaviors is for the formation of many theories about the self. The dynamics that exist between our mind modules and our left-brain interpreter module are responsible for the generation of human beliefs.

Once one becomes sensitive to how strongly behavior guides our beliefs and how they are formed, one becomes aware of the importance of the overarching social structure. Thus, an environment that conditions some of our mental modules to actions that may not be in the long-term best interests of our general belief systems ought to be avoided. For example, a belief in marital fidelity might be seriously challenged when at a Christmas party you find yourself succumbing to the attractive advances of someone new. That is, possible rewards from the environment could find their mark in one of the modules, which in turn generates a behavior. That behavior, once carried out, must be interpreted, and the new belief about the value of fidelity that results may well be at odds with other values. As we come to appreciate this process we gain a greater understanding of the biological basis of cultural phenomena.

Human brain research urges the view that our brains are organized in such a way that many mental systems coexist in what may be thought of as a confederation. The findings of this research also suggest that identifiable regions of the human brain allow for certain computations that make our species the only one capable of high-order, abstract inference, and that out of this special inference-making capacity comes the unique capacity to interpret our multiple self. These interpretations can actually create beliefs. The possession of beliefs is a mechanism our species uses to free itself from being in a simple reflexlike relation with the rewards and punishments of society. At the same time, when our interpretive brain, which generates our personal sets of beliefs, is overwhelmed by the magnitude and frequency of such rewards, it can fall victim to new beliefs that may form as a result of reflexively having to interpret the elicited behaviors.

Related to these principles of brain operation is the personal perception humans possess that they act of their own free will. Civilized, educated, twentieth-century humans, some even contrary to their working knowledge of modern physics, believe they are freely acting agents. Even habitual behaviors are viewed as freely willed. At a psychological level, Albert Einstein felt he was acting freely even though intellectually he was committed to the idea of a mechanistic universe. The belief that we act of our own free will is such a powerful one it must result from a basic feature of human brain organization. I propose that this belief follows from the modular theory of mind that will be explicated here. Since we are continually interpreting behaviors produced by independent brain modules as behaviors that are produced by the self, we come to the conclusion, which is largely illusionary, that we are acting freely. I will argue that it is this inescapable personal perception that finds our beliefs becoming altered the way they do in response to a variety of social forces.

In this book I explore with the reader the scientific evidence that has led me to these views. Much of the story is about the exciting discoveries of mental mechanisms as they have become more generally understood by our studies of the brain. But I hope to go beyond this to place those findings into a larger social context, a context that surely interacts with the physical nature of our species, but is one that is usually not addressed.

Basic cognitive phenomena, such as acquiring and holding social beliefs, are just as much a product of human brain organization as our desires to eat, sleep, and have sex. These special human properties of the mind are the result of brain organization, and as such reveal that many of the surface differences in cultural beliefs are the inevitable product of how the brain interprets the many milieus of this world. We know that the four or so billion people on this earth have the same type of brain and that our species has possessed this type of brain for at least forty thousand years. It is an awesome fact, one that gives me hope that by divining the brain's nature we will become enlightened about the mechanisms of belief formation and consequently more tolerant of the diversity of human beliefs.

Understanding the brain processes that lead to the formation and maintenance of belief systems gives us a foundation for understanding more clearly the basics of human mental life. But in order to accompany me on the journey through my experiences in brain research that lead up to these ideas, it is important for readers to grasp certain basic principles of brain organization, which I turn to now in chapter 2. Once these principles are understood, the larger issues of how the brain actually produces cognition and beliefs become a joy to discover.

CHAPTER 2

Basic Brain Principles

UNDERSTANDING the brain's relation to basic issues of human nature raises some deep questions about knowledge of the structure and function of that particular piece of biological tissue. The majority of scientists see the brain itself as endlessly modifiable and ever-responsive to environmental contingencies. To them, the mind of a human just born into the world is rather empty, but ready to be filled up and structured by the cultural environment. Those who hold such a view look with suspicion on findings that seem to suggest there are set properties to brain tissue that impose specific features on the mind. In order to learn more about how principles of brain organization relate to cognition, we must first learn something about certain main features of brain development and about their psychological correlates. In short, one needs to know what brain tissue is like. How does it work? How does it respond to experience? What limits does the nature of this tissue put on any theorizing about our species?

How such questions might be answered began to be revealed to me about twenty-five years ago when I read a most intriguing article in *Scientific American* written by my future mentor, Roger W. Sperry.[1] I was then an undergraduate at Dartmouth College. He was one of the foremost brain scientists in the world, the Hixon Professor of Psychobiology at the California Institute of Technology (Caltech). Sperry's article explored how nerve circuits grow to specific places in the brain. For example, how does a frog's optic nerve, the nerve that will carry information about what the frog sees, find its way from the eye to its proper connection in the brain? Any explanation of such matters must draw on the knowledge of how the brain is structured by the genetic code, and what are its limits for change in response to environmental events. Understanding how nerves grow is about as fundamental as things get in learning about the brain.

The 1960s were golden years for American science, when almost every reasonable research program could get funded. On what I thought was a long shot, I wrote to ask Sperry for a summer job between my junior and senior years. My home was close to Caltech, and I thought it would be perfect. To my surprise, he wrote back saying that it would not only be possible but that the National Science Foundation had summer fellowships for the likes of me. I couldn't believe it, but nonetheless managed to accept the offer. That summer proved to be the pivotal ten weeks of my life.

The lab was exceedingly cordial, and Sperry, who was already something of a legend, welcomed me with every courtesy. I was the lowest underling in the lab; but as in any large lab there were other underlings there who were generally available as companions and who taught me not only about the brain but about science in general. It was my good luck to get to know a most articulate and enthusiastic young psychologist, Mitchell Glickstein, who now, after years in American universities, is a professor at University College in London. Glickstein was doing fine work at Caltech but also was one of those memorable people who gave freely of his time to teach neophytes like me. He was, and still is, a wonderful scholar and teacher, and I learned much from him.

My first order of business was to become familiar with the early experiments done by Sperry. I was soon to learn that any biologically educated person is amazed by those who maintain the tabula rasa theory, that all brains start this life more or less the same. That idea, welded onto the American psyche by the Constitution, was forcefully argued in the intellectual community by the psychologist, John B. Watson. Watson was the recognized spokesman for an American reaction against German Rationalism and the fragility of introspective evidence when taken as scientific evidence.[2] His views came to rest on two major considerations. The first is that the manipulation of reward contingencies can be a powerful determinant of behavior, especially in animals. The second is that interaction with the environment gives the nervous system its structure. Watson made his case at a time when the brain sciences were young and scientists were largely ignorant of how the brain is built. In fact, it could be argued that when Watson was proposing his theories he was actually encouraged by contemporary biological research that the brain was infinitely plastic. At that time, in the early 1930s, the accepted view in brain science was that "function precedes form," that an arm had to be used as an arm before the neurons innervating the arm became specified for that purpose. In short, the biologic view was the equivalent of the psychologic view of the newborn organism being born with a clean slate.

Sperry's work helped to set things straight. He showed that the intricate neural networks that manage and control the appendages are established during development and are carefully formed and built under the control of genetic mechanisms. These circuits become set in their ways early in life and their capacities are strictly limited and defined at that time. The implication of this work on the peripheral nervous system is that many central circuits of the brain are the same, such that each person's individual nature reflects his or her underlying, genetically prescribed neural organization. How brains adopt psychological character depends not only on accidents of environmental events but also on their innate architecture.

This work began at the University of Chicago when Sperry,

still a graduate student, questioned the views of his famous mentor, Paul Weiss.[3] The thrust of Sperry's research was that nerves grow in prespecified ways to their destination points. Thus, contrary to Weiss's view, nerves grow out to a limb already centrally specified through genetically controlled mechanisms. Nerves do not grow out in a random way and then have the peripheral structure they happen onto specify what they do. Nerves are predestined to do particular jobs and they find the right peripheral tissues to connect with. For example, if in a rat the left hind leg nerve is experimentally diverted through surgical manipulation into the right hind leg, the right hind leg begins to act as if it were the left hind leg. And the situation remains this way for the life of the rat.[4]

In other classic experiments Sperry cut the optic nerve of a goldfish and studied how specifically it would grow back to the proper points of connection in the brain itself. Here, instead of looking at the specificity of nerves growing out of the central nervous system, he was assessing the kind of specificity for nerves growing into the central nervous system, the seat of important psychological processes. The regenerative process was most exact, with specific retinal points represented by particular neurons finding their way to definite regions in the fish's visual system. If the neurons were diverted into an incorrect area, they would grow through foreign zones and find the right part of the brain (see figure 2.1).

Sperry's model, which has now been verified through thousands of examples, is that "form precedes function."[5] Currently there are several theories about what the exact, biologic mechanism is by which a nerve knows where to grow. The identification of that mechanism is not settled.[6] No one, however, now doubts that the neuronal system develops under tight genetic control. Personal brain organization also is under tight genetic control and is not easily perturbable by environmental influence. Sperry showed that specific neuronal connections were made under direction of the genome, not the environment. And studying the

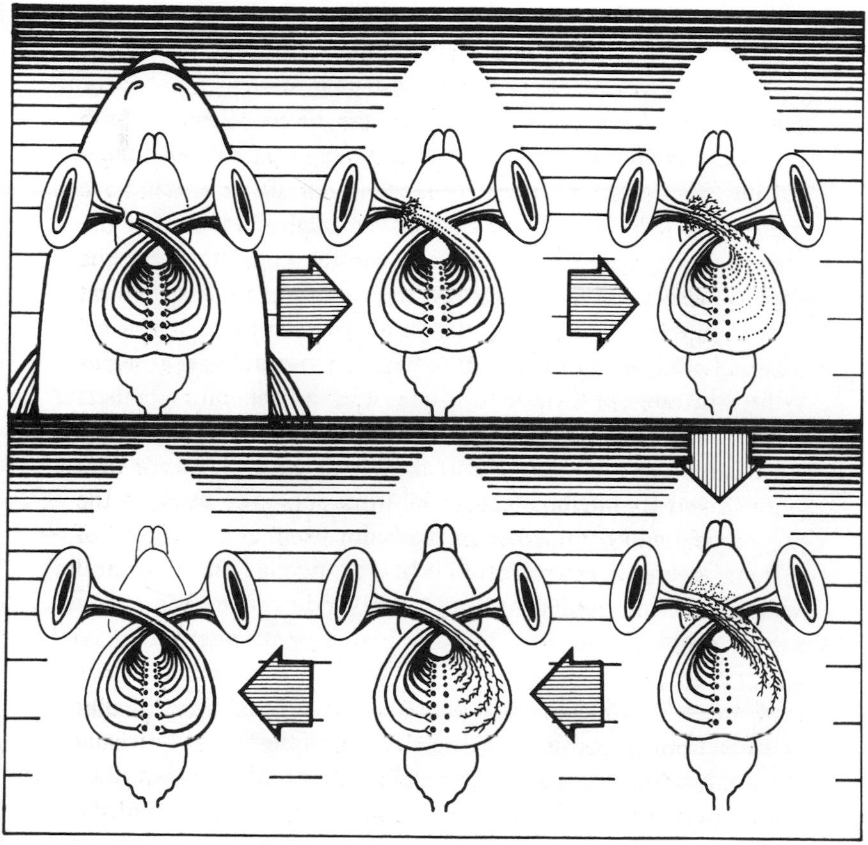

Figure 2.1. An example of Sperry's work on neurospecificity. The neurons from the fish eye that had been cut grow back to their proper, exact places in the brain, bypassing incorrect zones (start at top left and follow arrows).

issue, working with data, talking about the biologic context, gave all of us in Sperry's lab a deep respect for the genetic component in our lives.

It is also important to realize that a developing biologic system such as the nervous system is under tight, but not altogether complete, genetic control. A vast number of environmental influences arise around the organism—external forces of the mother as well as forces from the outside physical environment. The force of gravity causes water to flow downhill, but the water can be diverted from a seemingly predestined course by the judicious placement of a rock. In the biologic context of the brain, it is probably more accurate to say that with our present knowledge, most of these influences remain unspecified, but they are definitely there. Comparison of the brains of siblings, or perhaps even those of identical twins at a postmortem, reveals gross differences in morphology; the variations in the microstructure of the cell-to-cell organization are staggering. Since the brains of close cohorts are different, it is not difficult to imagine the wide range of variation in the rest of the population. Whereas everybody has a left and a right hemisphere, a midbrain, and a visual cortex, the proportion of cells in each of these systems and how they interconnect varies from person to person.

An intriguing thought is to consider whether the brain variations among individuals underlie the psychological variations among normal adults. Although everybody responds to rewards, for example, some people respond with greater intensity. Could this difference in intensity be reflected in a differential projection of neurons to a part of the brain that mediates the chemical mechanism responsible for the effect? In other words, do people who are exquisitely sensitive to flattery or the appreciation of external goods have brains with a larger than usual projection to the reward system of the brain?

With genetics supplying the main framework for neural growth and development, it is now recognized that there are definite time periods during development when brain organization is modifiable. These periods for change are short and are presently known for only a few species and a few kinds of experience. Some of the best examples come from studies on the cat's visual system. In Nobel-Prize-winning research, Harvard neurophysiologists David Hubel and Torsten Wiesel described the normal cellular architecture of the visual cortex.[7] They discovered that in both the adult and newborn cat an identical organization exists, consisting of predetermined proportions of cells that respond to particular orientation of light and dark edges presented in the cat's real field of vision. Some cells respond to leftward leaning lines, some to rightward, some to vertical, some to horizontal, and some to other orientations found in between these extremes. Other features include the number of cells that receive information from just one eye as opposed to both eyes.

Since the pioneering studies carried out in the 1960s, a number of subsequent investigators have shown that there is a time period during the first weeks of a kitten's life when exposure to an abnormal visual environment can change the proportion of cells committed to detecting lines of a particular orientation. Thus, if a new kitten sees only lines of a vertical orientation during the first three weeks of life, more cells will respond to lines of that orientation when the kitten is tested at ten weeks of age. Lines or edges presented in nonvertical orientations will tend not to elicit any responses. Presenting such environmental manipulations a few weeks later in a cat's life, say, at ten weeks of age, seems to have no effect on the normal organization of the visual system. The critical period is over. The brain system seems set for the duration of the cat's life (see figure 2.2).

Another example of these phenomena, one of my favorites, comes from the work of Rockefeller University Professor Fernando Nottebohm.[8] A young male bird learns his song from the adult male. If the young male is exposed to song anytime before he is a year old, he learns the proper song. If he does not hear the song until after he is a year old, he is never able to learn it. The critical period for learning bird song, then, lasts for one year. This period of learning is not unlike those for humans during the development of their language and speech. If a young child does not acquire language by a particular time, it never develops normally.

Another way to look at the relation between brain growth and psychological development is to examine parallels between the order of acquisition of childhood skills and the breakdown of

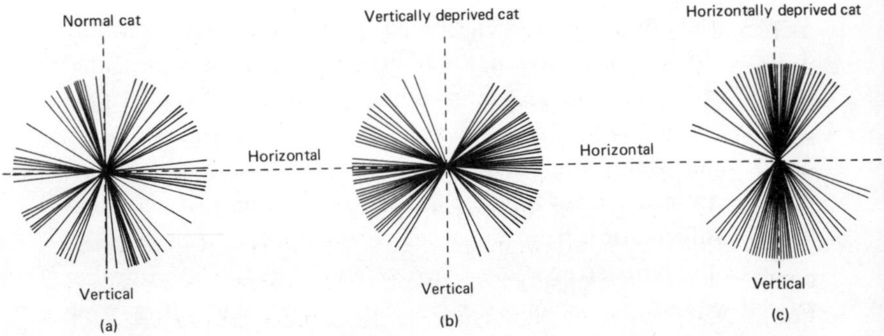

Figure 2.2 Orientation of lines that elicit a response from cells in the visual cortex of a cat under three conditions. In (a) the normal distribution of responses is shown. In (b) the responses are shown for a cat raised in an environment with only horizontal lines, and in (c) the responses of a cat raised having seen only vertical lines. Brain organization can be influenced early in life. If the exposure occurs at ten weeks, however, these brain changes are not possible.

such skills after acquired brain lesions occur in adulthood. Parallel deficits may suggest that areas of the brain where damage in the adult results in loss of a particular function are the same areas that need to mature in the young brain in order to support that function. An example will make this clear.

It has been shown that in young rats a specific brain area called the dentate gyrus of the hippocampus is immature for the first month after birth.[9] When these animals are carefully studied, the young rats are seen to behave like adult rats with lesions in this area. In humans this brain area, the dentate gyrus, matures after birth as well. As in the rat, the corresponding behavioral abilities of the preschool child are not yet wholly functioning until the critical brain areas mature. Thus, there are parallels between the behavioral abilities possible when a structure is lacking either maturationally or because of a lesion. This suggests that particular brain regions must reach a certain level of maturity before the behavior they mediate can be achieved. Ages five to seven appear to be the key period.

The discovery of such mechanisms is interesting from a number of vantages. First, the data show how real environmental input can modify the genetic intent of an organism. The other side of the coin, however, suggests that the conditions under which such changes can be effected are limited and short-lived. Both points are of extreme importance.

There are other important features of the developing brain to consider. The rate of growth varies from one brain to another. For example, Billy may have more of his cortical cells myelinated than Bobby has by the age of one year. Myelin is the substance that wraps around neurons and gives them each a sheath. This sheath changes the microstructure of the neuron and enables the neuron to transmit its electrical impulses more efficiently. Without this sheath the neuron is sluggish, which is an important consideration when dealing with an intriguing aspect of brain development, the myelinization of the cerebral cortex. Much of human cognitive activity takes place in the cortex. For the cortex to work efficiently, the myelin must be in place. Yet, myelinization develops slowly.[10] Some regions of the brain do not receive their full complement until the third decade. Again, this fact raises interesting questions about the brain correlates of developing psychological processes.

It is widely assumed by developmental psychologists that various cognitive stages must be realized in a specified order for normal cognition to occur. Ability A must be usable before ability B can mature, B must be usable before C can mature, and so on. Psychologists of every persuasion argue over the nature and quality of each of these mental abilities, but they all tend to believe that each step must be completed in its proper order. As a consequence, psychological models of development are created and are discussed as if this psychological process were the basic building unit for personal cognition.

A biological view that also honors the unique character of psychological experience could argue this issue of the building process by claiming nothing happens at the psychological level until the brain areas subserving the requisite psychological processes are connected and functioning. Just as a computer that has a finite capacity cannot process more information than it has memory chips to handle, the developing organism can do only so much of a psychological job with the neuronal hardware it has functioning. When the organism achieves another level of capacity, however, the argument would be that the brain has matured—more cortical areas have become active or more efficient, making the new psychological ability possible. One biologic possibility for this further development in the human is the differential myelinization pattern in the human cerebrum. The myelinization process is a delayed one and matures only in the brain areas most responsible for cognition at about the time a particular skil! is realized in a young child.

Another important principle about the developing brain is that, when all is said and done, all studies to date have shown that environmental influences affect the brain only in a negative way. This fact stands in marked contrast to the claims about the importance of early environment, much of which come from brain researchers themselves. The only time in the natural history of an organism that it is operating at its full, undisturbed genetic potential is following an uneventful birth. This full neural deck, as it were, becomes diluted only by physical events impinging on the brain. Head injury, endocrine imbalances, nutritional adversities, all act negatively. Contrary to what many claim, there are no convincing data that an enriched environment can change brain power positively. This point is worth considering in some detail.

Many scientists were pleased when a group of biopsychologists started reporting in the 1960s that rats raised in an enriched environment as compared to control rats had thicker, more complex cortical neural circuitry.[11] The claim was that their brains were better and more capable of carrying out problem solving. Those who believe strongly in the influences of environment, a view shared by those people that more or less "own" the primary and secondary school establishments, were thrilled and used this new "biologic data" to argue for greater control over early environment. Implicit in their rhetoric was the idea that superkids could be created. Suddenly the environmentally minded abandoned their usual distrust of biologic statements that suggest each of us has a predestined limited capacity, and they instead argued on the strength of this supposed biologic data that the brain capacity could be enhanced.

Since these studies began, the experimenters themselves have not lost their faith in these claims, which is a normal circumstance. The neurobiologic community at large, however, is less sanguine. First, the studies had and continue to have a basic design flaw. The so-called enriched animals are compared to so-called normal litter mates. But what is called enriched is most likely normal and what is called normal is most likely deprived. What the experimenters do is place one group in an environment full of toys and colors and they frequently handle them. In short, the animals receive stimulation. They experience something like a normal environment. The control or nonstimulated rats, on the other hand, stay in a small rat cage in a strict environmentally controlled animal room and basically lead a deprived life. Baselines are relative, and in this case the baseline was mislabeled.

The second major development in developmental neurobiology that undercuts the view that experience enhances cortical growth is the discovery that the developing brain overinnervates all areas.[12] This means that if brain area A sends projections to brain area B, those projections in the young brain can be seven times denser than projections existing in the adult brain. It is not yet known how and why neurons succeed in establishing proper connections in the appropriate brain areas, but it is known that brain development starts out rapidly and then slows down.

But because the developing brain is so delicate, it can be slowed down early on by an interruption or injury. This has been clearly shown at the clinical level. Brain injury to either hemisphere during the childhood years causes a marked decrease in verbal IQ.[13] This conclusion is based on comparison of the verbal IQ range of an injured child with the verbal IQ range of his or her siblings. Relative to them, the injured child is severely impaired, a statistic that is at odds with the usual family profile of IQ for siblings.

An important aspect of this developmental data on IQ is that the detrimental effect of experiencing an early head injury is more acutely apparent if the injury occurs before the age of one. Injuries occurring after this age have less effect on verbal IQ. This observation, which is a robust clinical finding, unveils another complex and intriguing feature of brain development. The very immature brain is in such a delicate dynamic state that any insult to its growth pattern disrupts its ultimate upward potential. While the injury is occurring at a time when the brain is presumed to be most capable of self-repair, it is simultaneously a time when the brain is most vulnerable to any interruption of normal growth. At the same time, the effects of an injury occurring anytime after the first year have less to do with general intelligence and more to do with specific skills. This means that at a very early age, the specialized functions of each half-brain are expressing themselves and with brain injury are irreparably damaged or lost.

What emerges is a picture of a brain that is a mosaic of neural centers behaving in delicate and dynamic interrelation during the early years. The parts of the brain that are not responsible for the management of adult cognitive skills are very active in establishing these cognitive processes in particular brain areas during development. The brain is aswirl with activity. Yet just as quickly as it starts, this activity stops when the specialized capacities of the adult have reached their final stage. When the brain system has reached maturity, changes in its abilities appear restricted to its capacity to learn, and this capacity differs from person to person.

After the early years of development, by the time of a person's adolescence, the brain becomes neurologically set. Its long connecting circuits transmit information in specified ways, and injury to these circuits causes permanent impairment. This is not to say that no recovery is possible. What is at issue with cases of injury, however, is the mechanism of improvement. It appears likely that undamaged brain areas begin to regulate the behavior that has been disrupted or lost, usually by applying a new behavioral strategy. Thus, what appears to be brain repair is not recovery of damaged brain tissue, but adaptation by tissue that has not been damaged. That is the "hard" view. Some are more hopeful in neuroscience. I am not.

And how is the mature, normally developed brain organized? What is the structural logic that allows it to do the kind of tasks we humans do so well?

When I started doing brain research in the early 1960s, the brain was considered a much simpler organ than ensuing research has shown it to be. It was assumed then that sensory pathways conveyed sensory information to the cortex and there, in association areas, the information combined with other processes to organize neural messages to be sent to the motor or response part of the brain.[14] With few exceptions there was a pervasive "stimulus and response" mentality to both brain science and much of psychology. The psychological view was strangling the field of cognition. The biological view was static, waiting for new techniques. These techniques were developed, and now after thousands of studies, they have revealed in a profound sense how the adult brain is organized.[15] And the advances in defining the adult brain over the past several years have been most remarkable.

It has been said that the "gain in brain is mainly in the stain." In the early 1970s new chemical stains were developed that allowed more sensitive tracking of neuronal pathways; new structural relations were discovered. This discovery, combined with an ever-evolving set of neurophysiological techniques, unearthed the new logic about brain organization.

Until this time the brain was viewed as a single integrated system that gave rise to a unified cognitive process. Sensory information was projected to one part of the brain for any particular modality such as vision. Upon arriving in the brain, the information was elaborated in visual association areas; and from these areas a message was somehow sent to the equally discretely defined motor system, allowing for an appropriate response. This sensory information was analyzed to a greater degree at each stage along the way. Thus, at the first stage of the visual process, brain cells responded only to simple primitive visual stimuli such as edges or corners. As cells were stimulated in deeper levels of the brain's visual system, where more complex computations were possible, responses to more specific features of the visual world were generated. The notion was actually proposed that cells in some part of the advanced visual areas responded to such specific things as pictures of hands, or brushes, or faces; as a result they became known as "grandmother cells," or cells that would specifically respond to particular stimuli, such as one's grandmother.

With the aid of new stains and other techniques, it was discovered that the primary visual information coming in from a sensory surface such as the retina projected to a variety of places in the brain. To be sure, their primary projections were to the already well-recognized primary areas. But the new cell stains revealed important secondary projections (see figure 2.3). This raised the question of what animals would see if the primary projections were destroyed, leaving intact only the secondary projection areas. Experiments were performed on all kinds of animals. On humans, the effects of naturally occurring lesions to the primary visual system were observed. The results were uniformly striking. Animals could see complex stimuli without their primary visual systems. The earlier notion of a linear path of sensory information into more and more complex constructions finally terminating in the perception of a discrete object underwent revision. There was a redundancy quotient to brain

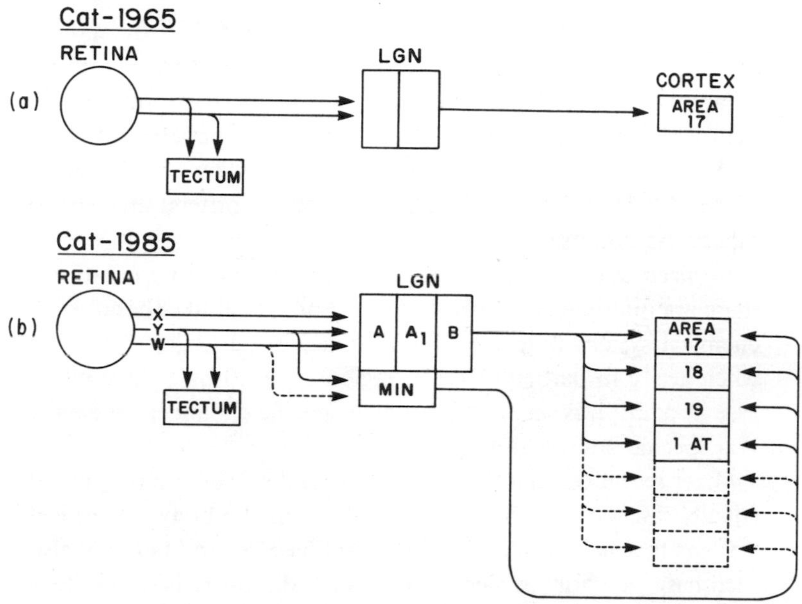

Figure 2.3 In (a) the hierarchical view of the organization of the visual system is depicted. In recent years this view has given way to the one indicated in (b), where the visual system is multiply represented and incoming fibers are projected to many brain zones simultaneously.

organization. Sensory information is now viewed as being multiply represented in separate and somewhat independent processing modules.[16] The actual mechanism by which one sees one's grandmother, in both real life and in the mind's eye, remains elusive. For present purposes, it is important to appreciate that the adult brain is not organized as a unitary monolithic system, with each part linked to every other in some kind of hierarchical way. In short, instead of information being processed serially, it now is clear there is much parallel processing.

While anatomists have been discovering the complexity of the basic neural architecture, neurochemists have been unearthing multitudes of specific chemicals that allow one neuron to "talk" to another.[17] These chemicals, which are secreted by the axonal tip of neurons, change the chemical milieu in and around adjacent neurons. This chemical change is what allows the neuronal message to pass from one neuron to another. Modern brain research shows that particular neurons are responsive to certain kinds of chemicals (called neurotransmitters) and not to others. As a consequence of these complex findings, it is now recognized that in addition to multiple sensory representations, there are multiple chemical systems. And, in all likelihood, each chemical system is specifically involved in particular functions when active in particular brain regions. Parkinson's disease is a case in point. It is accompanied by a specific chemical deficiency in a specific brain region.

Other recent correlative neurochemical discoveries have proved equally fascinating. These have to do with the body's chemical systems that help modulate pain and pleasure, and perhaps also such basic activities as sleep.[18] One such discovery is of the well-publicized, self-produced opiates called endorphins which are crucial to a body's well-being. These chemicals are activated under conditions of bodily stress and serve to curb some of the pain we would otherwise feel in their absence. There is no doubt that we would feel more pain without them. A drug called Naloxone blocks the action of these self-produced opiates and, if it is administered after heavy exercise or a painful stimulus, the discomfort is greatly increased.

These advances in brain research and related fields are of major importance to the understanding of how the brain functions, and any interested reader should investigate them further to learn more of the considerable details. For my purposes here, I just want my readers to be aware of their existence. They tell us that physical and identifiable brain mechanisms are governing some of our most personal experiences. They tell us that at some basic level environmental contingencies do work because they elicit specific brain action. But they also tell us that the brain itself regulates these actions and can modulate or enhance their intensity. These modulating influences are possible most clearly in human beings, where the existence of belief systems can override primitive brain responses to environmentally induced painful and pleasurable events.

Another important brain principle is that the amount of pain and pleasure an organism can experience is finite. The chemical systems that mediate these functions are finite. They reach a peak, and attempts to elicit responses to more of the stimulation in question are wasted effort. Finally, especially in this domain, individual differences are enormous. One person's level for pain may be another's level for only mild discomfort. The same is true for pleasure. Recent studies are showing that these individual variations are most likely due to different structural capacities in a person's brain. Jones's capacity to make endorphins may be different from Smith's or his capacity to respond to the self-made chemicals may be different. The possibilities for explaining so many dimensions of personality are breathtaking.

My short tutorial is over. I hope I have imparted some understanding of the nature of the brain. These few glimpses of basic brain mechanisms are sufficient to tell us what we need to know about the basic nature of the tissue. Four principles emerge: (a) the brain develops under tight genetic control; (b) its basic architecture can be modified only very early in life and then only in a negative way; (c) it is organized in such a way that relatively independent processing modules exist everywhere throughout the brain system; and (d) it has methods of self-modulating influences from the environment through an intricate, self-governed brain chemical system.

That summer of 1960 convinced me that brain science, especially in terms of behavior, would be my life's work. I assumed that I would finish my premed studies and trot off to medical school as everyone expected me to. Back in Hanover, however, life was not the same. I couldn't get the summer experience out of my mind. Finally I wrote Sperry and asked if he would sponsor an application for me to do graduate studies with him. He said he would be delighted, and so largely through his support I was admitted to Caltech the following summer.

This change wasn't the easiest thing to explain to my father, a physician passionately involved with medicine. My brother was in medical school at the time and I was expected to follow suit. My father, who had been born into a large Italian family, thought medicine was one of the most honorable professions a man could pursue. He kept telling me that I couldn't realize this until I actually practiced it. He had gone to medical school because, upon his graduation from St. Anselm's in New Hampshire, the monsignor had called him in and told him he should go to Loyola in Chicago. Although it was late June, the monsignor had said he would make all of the arrangements. My father protested, saying he had never even taken chemistry in college. The monsignor said, "So what? Learn it over the summer, and while you are at it learn a little physics. The boys in Chicago think you have." He added, winking, "and you had better not make a liar out of me. I also told them you were seventh in your class. I didn't tell him there were only seven in the class." This method of gaining admission to medical school is no longer available, but I am not at all sure that the current methods are any wiser. My father, by all accounts, was an extraordinary surgeon. When I told him about my change in plans he merely smiled and muttered something to the effect that he thought this might be the case. Then he said, "Whatever you want is okay by me. I just don't understand why you would want to be a Ph.D. when you can always hire one." He had me there.

CHAPTER 3

Split-Brain Studies: The Early Years

THERE IS an axiom in biological circles stating that if you want to understand how something works, you study it functioning in disrepair. If a trained scientist were confronted with a television set for the first time and asked to figure out how it works, the task would be easier if the set did not function properly. With the picture fluttering, hypotheses could be immediately formed about its underlying composition, and the scientist would be on the way to understanding how it works.

The same approach can be used to understand how the human brain generates and sustains normal human cognition. The neurologic patient suffering from a disease that disrupts normal brain relations can generate rich insights into basic brain organization. More important, the study of the disrupted brain teaches us how the cognitive system itself is normally organized. As a consequence, neurologic patients produce information at two levels. They tell us about brain principles and about cognitive principles. This field of endeavor is formally called cognitive neuroscience, and research in this area has occupied most of my time for the past twenty-five years. Much of this work is pivotal to my present arguments.

In brief, research on the neurologic patient will allow claims to be made about certain crucial features of brain organization and personal cognition. As I've already mentioned, it will become clear that, contrary to our intense introspections, consciousness is not an indivisible unitary process. Instead, what appears to be personal conscious unity is the product of a vast array of separate and relatively independent mental systems that continually process information from both the human internal and external environment. Put in more general terms, the human mind is more of a sociological entity than a psychological entity. That is, the human mind is composed of a vast number of more elementary units, and many of these units are capable of carrying out rather sophisticated mental work. These activities can go on outside the awareness of our verbal conscious system. Putting it the other way around, extensive information processing in the brain is going on independent of verbal processes. Further, the management of these separate systems is the chore of the normally dominant computational systems of the left half-brain.

What also emerges from recent research is that these left-brain computational systems are closely tied to language processes but are not the language system per se. It is the appreciation of these aspects of brain organization that suggest new insights into how mental phenomena such as personal beliefs are formed and maintained, and how, as a result of their reflexive presence in the human mind, the simple effects of external contingencies can be overruled. The bulk of the work suggesting these views comes from split-brain research, and I will begin, logically, at the beginning.

That summer at Caltech in 1960, I learned about Sperry's other discovery, the split-brain animal. The term was coined to describe a surgical procedure performed on cats and monkeys that disconnected the left brain, or hemisphere, from the right brain, or hemisphere. In the initial experiments carried out in the early 1950s by Ronald Myers (who was then a student of Sperry's) and Sperry, the aim was to isolate the neural pathways by which visual information presented to one hemisphere was integrated with that presented to the other.[1] In order to understand what I am saying, the reader has to consider only the page he or she is reading. Fixate on any letter or word (figure 3.1). The human brain, as well as the brains of the cat and monkey, is organized in such a way that visual information to the left of the fixated point is projected to the right brain while all visual information falling to the right of the fixated point is projected to the left brain. Yet, you see the visual world as one integrated whole. Myers and Sperry wanted to find out which pathways were responsible for that integration. They found that out and much more.

The band that connects the two half-brains in mammals is called the corpus callosum. It is an enormous tract of nerve fibers (over two hundred million individual neurons in humans) and it is easily approachable for surgical sectioning. Severing this connection as well as a smaller, more anterior structure called the anterior commissure isolates one hemisphere from the other. Well, that is almost true. If, in addition, a structure called the optic chiasm is sectioned in the midline, visual information presented to one eye is projected to only one half-brain. Sectioning the chiasm is carried out only in animal research (see figure 3.2).

Myers and Sperry discovered that when the corpus callosum, anterior commissure, and optic chiasm were sectioned, visual discriminations taught to one brain were not known by the other. For example, if a cat learned while the right eye was open but the left was closed that every time it pushed a panel with a triangle on it, it would receive some liver paté, it did not know that fact subsequently when the left eye was open and the right was closed. The information learned by the right brain did not transfer over to the left brain. In study after study, animals with sectioned neural interconnections between the hemispheres behaved as if they had two separate brains, hence the term "split-brain."[2]

Think for a moment what the implications are for humans.

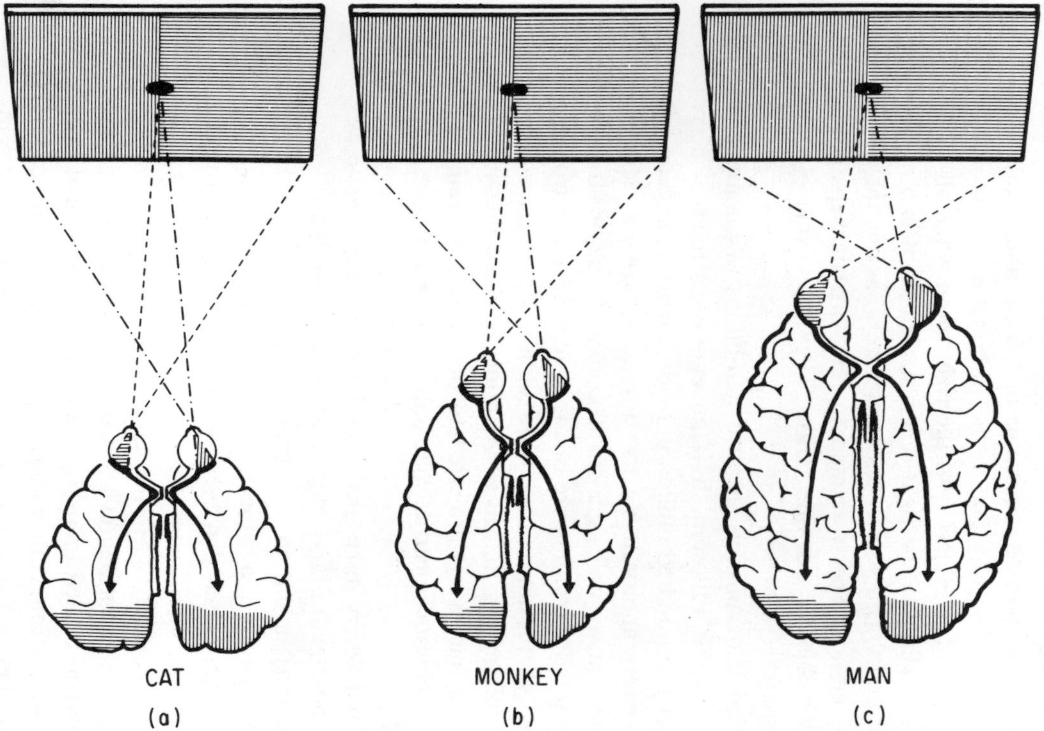

Figure 3.1. The vertebrate nervous system is organized in approximately the same fashion for all three species seen here. In (a) and (b) the cat and monkey look at a point. Everything to the left of the fixated point is projected to the right brain and vice versa. The same is true for man (c), which makes possible the separate testing of each half-brain after split-brain surgery. To simplify testing procedures in animals, the optic chiasm is sectioned.

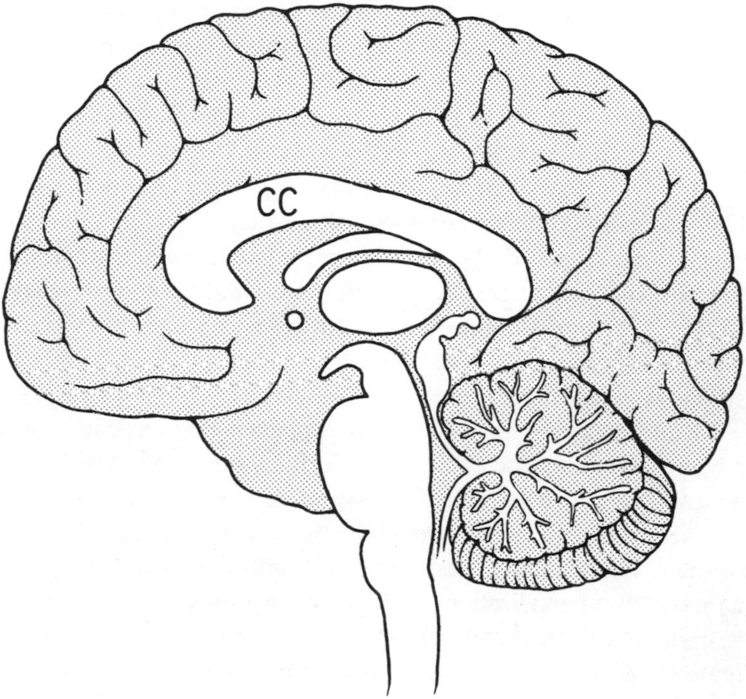

Figure 3.2 This is a sagittal view of a human brain. The large fiber tract (CC) is the corpus callosum. It is this structure that the neurosurgeon sections in seeking control for otherwise intractable epilepsy.

Fixate a point on the wall and hold your fixation. Now imagine I place to the left of fixation two objects, one an apple and one an orange. Keep fixating and imagine I tiptoe over and place a one hundred dollar bill under the apple, all of this going on to the left of fixation. Now close your eyes and just think for a moment about which piece of fruit I baited. If you pick up the correct fruit when you open your eyes, you may keep the one hundred dollars. If you now open your eyes and the fruit is still to the left of fixation, you would know the answer because the same hemisphere that saw me place the one hundred dollars under the apple is now being asked about it. If, however, I moved the apple and orange while your eyes were closed so that when you opened your eyes they now appeared to the right of fixation, the fruit would be seen by the left brain. That would present no problem for the normal brain. Surely the reader would still know what to do, since the band of fibers that connects the two hemispheres is still in place. Yet, the animal experiments suggested that if the neural interconnections between the two half-brains were cut, the left brain would not know what to do. This seemed unbelievable, and in fact no one believed it. Our everyday sense of what conscious unity is all about is so strong we would tend to reject such a claim.

There was a way to test it. It so happened that back in 1940 a neurosurgeon in Rochester, New York, by the name of William Van Wagenen had sectioned the neural connections between the two hemispheres in twenty-six epileptic patients. Epilepsy occurs in many kinds and degrees, and it is commonly managed with anticonvulsant medications. When medications fail to control it, epilepsy can frequently be brought under control by surgical removal of the brain tissue that is malfunctioning and triggering the seizures. In order for this procedure to work without causing more problems than it cures, the diseased area, or focus, has to be localized to a particular point in the brain, and that point cannot be in a crucial brain area such as the major language area. Since the focus is frequently not in a critical area, surgical removal can take place and the seizures controlled. But if the focus is in the language area, or if there are several foci, this method of medical relief is not possible; in such cases, split-brain surgery is considered.

In split-brain surgery, the corpus callosum is sectioned in either one or two stages. In the initial surgeries carried out by Van Wagenen, the anterior commissure was sometimes sectioned as well. The initial idea of the surgery was that by disconnecting the two half-brains, seizure activity initiated in one hemisphere would not spread to the other, thereby leaving one half-brain seizure-free and in control of the body.

These patients were observed at the time of their surgeries by a talented young neurologist, Andrew Akelaitis.[3] In a series of studies, Dr. Akelaitis reported that the patients seemed essentially normal or unchanged. Cutting the largest fiber tract in the brain appeared to create in humans no problems of integration between the two hemispheres. In fact, it was partly Akelaitis's studies that led Karl Lashley, the great neuropsychologist, to conclude that the most important aspect of brain organization was the overall amount of brain tissue present, not the specific areas. Cutting the brain interconnections and finding no change in function was about the biggest result for human clinical neurology in those days.

But something just didn't fit. The results of the animal work were clear, and though contrary, the Akelaitis work seemed just as clear. As I sat in freezing Hanover that last winter, I thought it would be a good idea to go test the Rochester patients. We had all talked about the patients during the preceding summer, and no one could figure out why the results were not like those seen in the animal studies. Were humans different or was the original testing flawed in some systematic way? I wrote to Sperry with some testing ideas involving Polaroid lenses and tachistoscopes. The problem was that in order to test the patients correctly, information presented to either the left or right of fixation had to be quick-flashed. A tachistoscope does just that. Sperry wrote back and said he liked the idea, made some suggestions, and wished me luck. I applied for a small grant from the Mary Hitchcock Foundation at the college to cover travel expenses during my stay in Rochester over the spring break and got one hundred dollars. A friend of mine was going to put me up so the money went straight to Hertz.

Everyone knew about the patients but no one had gotten around to actually testing them. Akelaitis had died as a young man and Van Wagenen had moved to Florida, so I was referred to another neurosurgeon. When I talked to him on the phone from Hanover he was cordial and receptive. He told me he had most of the patients' records and that by going through them I should be able to get names, addresses, and so on. I was to go to his office when I got to town and go to work.

After much preparation, I loaded the tachistoscopes, tape recorder, and other baggage, all borrowed from the psychology department of Dartmouth, into my rented car and took off. I was nervous about the whole thing.

I arrived in Rochester and went straight to the doctor's office. He was out, so his nurse directed me to the records and said I was to start. I took a stack of folders and began, trying to cut through a lot of what to me seemed like mumbo jumbo. After a couple of hours the phone rang. It was the neurosurgeon calling to tell me he had changed his mind and that I couldn't carry out the studies after all. I was flabbergasted. He gave no real reason but added, "You know I was a resident at the time those surgeries were carried out and, if you ask me, the callosum was rarely if ever fully sectioned."

I wrote Sperry the bad news, put away my gear, and played all spring. When I arrived in Pasadena in June, I knew immediately that I was in the right place. Many of the friends I had made the preceding summer were still there. I felt the added excitement of starting on a new adventure and the matter-of-fact curiosity of whether or not I could cope with the Caltech curriculum. I was appropriately nervous but nonetheless still sort of cocky. My first two years at Dartmouth were rocky times for me, and my "bucolic" California high school education wasn't behind me until the start of my junior year. At this point I felt I had a good Ivy League education and that once learning how to learn was in hand, the rest would be easy—or so I thought.

In order to qualify for a Ph.D. in biology one had to take an oral exam in zoology. I had just finished my comprehensive exams in zoology at Dartmouth and had done well, so I asked Sperry if I could take the test at the end of the summer and get it out of the way. He agreed and I prepared for a late summer exam to be given by Sperry and A. H. Sturdevant, the famous and very senior geneticist. I checked with the other graduate students about the test, and they told me Sturdevant had several boxes of insects he lent out for study—on the exam he gave a test box of fifty insects to identify by both genus and species. So I trotted up to his office, got the boxes, and retired to my office to study them.

The exam took place one afternoon in Sturdevant's office. He was an avuncular sort, always smoking a pipe. He led off the questioning and sure enough the first thing he asked me to do was identify a box of fifty insects. I got forty-nine out of the fifty correct. He smiled, asked me a couple of other perfunctory questions, and then passed the questioning over to Sperry. Sperry, who always adopts a stoic posture in this kind of situation, started off with the simplest question in embryology, one any undergraduate knows the answer to. He asked me to describe the development of the otic capsule, that is, the development of the inner ear. A piece of cake, I thought to myself, and started in. Sperry gave me no feedback. He just sat there and listened to my answer. There were no "Uh-huhs" or "yea, yea, yeas," no sign I was on the right track. I panicked. What the old otic capsule did in its proper migration to the correct part of the brain was to take a left turn, change its basic composition, and wind up, I think, in the liver. But after my answer they would have bet I couldn't recognize a frog if it had jumped up on the table. They asked me to step out of the room and a few minutes later Sperry came out to say they thought I ought to take the exam over in the fall after school started. I was crestfallen but wiser. So much for the Ivy League—Caltech would require my total energies.

Roger W. Sperry was forty-eight years old when I arrived. He had already survived a major medical incident, a bout with tuberculosis. Sperry was considered a complex figure, painfully shy and incessantly wondering what motivated people's actions. He was considered aloof by his peers, yet was entirely approachable by his students. Prior to his arrival at Caltech in the early 1950s at the insistence of Nobel laureate George Beadle, who accurately perceived his genius, Sperry had held some secondary positions in the academic world. Except perhaps for Sir John Eccles, Roger Sperry was far and away the most famous brain scientist living at the time. As a result of his revolutionary studies on nerve specificity, he was considered one of the primary thinkers in neurobiology. The data-driven theory he outlined in the 1950s still guides a huge amount of current research in neurobiology. He had also conducted a series of experiments setting limits on runaway theories about the underlying biology of Gestalt principles. And he had been working on the split-brain preparation for approximately eight years. He was an institution in his own time.

Meanwhile the real business I was interested in had already started. Shortly after I arrived, Sperry called me in to say that Joseph Bogen, a neurosurgical resident at the White Memorial Hospital, was planning to do split-brain surgery on humans late that fall. Bogen had been at Caltech on a postdoctoral fellowship with Professor Anthony Van Harreveld whose office was next to Sperry's. Bogen had become interested in the split-brain issue and wanted to see whether or not the surgery made sense for the control of epilepsy in humans. The earlier reports by Van Wagenen and Akelaitis were always quoted as showing the seizure-control aspect of the surgery to be inconsequential. Bogen dug out all the papers and began trying to check out this assertion. He discovered that when all the case histories were sorted out, there was just as much evidence confirming control as there was for nonconfirmation. Bogen thought the surgery worth a try, especially on a patient who could not be controlled through normal anticonvulsant medication. Case W.J. was the first patient.

Since I had already developed some tests for the Rochester experiments and since I was just starting out, Sperry thought I was a good choice to head the project. There were others around who could have done the work but they were either leaving or uninterested. Mitchell Glickstein had tried his luck on a girl who had been referred to the lab with a suspected callosal lesion. The testing proved impossible and he decided he liked monkeys better, so the project fell straight into my lap.

One of the things that made Sperry an excellent mentor was that he left you alone. He set a laboratory context for work, and he was always there working to make things better, to advise, to assist, and to guide. But he didn't order anyone around or tell anyone what to do. Many senior scientists do not operate their labs that way: graduate students are pawns for their chess games. Not Sperry, and because of that everybody benefited—Sperry as much as his students. As a result, everything that came out of the work was a real team effort. We all freely interacted and talked all the time about everything. In the early years the work was being done primarily by Sperry, Bogen, and myself, but others were around too.

In the early 1960s, when all of this was going on, there was a special atmosphere at Caltech. For the first year I lived in a house across the street from the biology labs, which was whimsically listed in the local phone book as J. A. Prufrock. Charles Hamilton, another student of Sperry's, arranged that I got a room there, right across the hall from his. Five people were living in the house at the time, including two theoretical physicists who have gone on to great things.

Sidney Coleman, then a student of the great Richard Feynman and now a professor of theoretical physics at Harvard, lived down the hall. His work habits were as odd as mine. At one point I used to get up at midnight and go to the lab until about four in the morning, come back for a break, and then go back to the lab until about six in the evening. One morning I came back about four and Coleman's light was on. There he was lying on his bed, staring straight up at the ceiling. This was late even for him, so I stuck my head in his room and said, "Sidney, are you all right?" "Quiet," he said, "I'm working."

Norman Dombey, a Britisher and prize student of Nobel Prize–winning theoretical physicist Murray Gell-Mann, was always walking around as if lost in thought. It was nerve-racking because Dombey understood things I couldn't even spell. One day after beating him in a game of chess, an event I relished, I said, "Norman, what is it you are thinking about all the time? It's distressing to see you apparently working every minute." Dombey, who if sent to the store would have a hard time coming home with a loaf of bread, looked at me quite startled and said, "Why, my dear man, I am usually trying to remember whether Chuck remembered to buy my Coca-Cola!"

At the Prufrock, parties were frequent and many professors came over for the fun. Coleman used to say, when he was really feeling cocky, that the only difference between Feynman and himself that he could detect was that at the physics seminars Feynman's hand always went up for the key question exactly thirty milliseconds before his own. One night, after the split-brain work was off the ground, Feynman came over to one of the parties. He knew about everything that was going on, and so on the way out he said to Hamilton and me, "If you guarantee me I can do physics after split-brain surgery, you can split me. Maybe I could do even more." I said, "It's guaranteed," and we all laughed. Feynman paused for a moment, then said, "Well, good night," and stuck out both hands for adieus.

Joe Bogen was always around. He is a big man with a huge appetite for life. Sperry was not much of a café person, but Bogen was a chum and loved to eat, drink, and talk about everything. He introduced me to good wines, good food, and good conversation. He is bright, extremely articulate, and full of energy. Several times during those early years we did things that paid off simply because Bogen kept pushing us.

It was more than a smart crowd. It was a group of people

who were there to accomplish great things and there was no way one was going to settle for anything less. We all worked hard and, because of the special Caltech atmosphere, we all felt special. I guess Caltech thought so too. The day I received my draft notice in the fall of 1961, I took it in to the chairman's office as was the set routine. That afternoon I got a call from the local draft board saying it would not be necessary to come in. It was unquestionably an elitist atmosphere. They were the best of times.

There is always an asymmetry in relationships with physical scientists. One needs to know too much to say anything intelligent about their work. Fortunately, they can comment on your work with greater ease. One needs to know only a few basic points about human brain anatomy in order to follow the line of research to be outlined, and this is what allows me to tell my story more generally. As I have described earlier with regard to animals, our species also possesses two cerebral hemispheres, or half-brains. The left cortex, or hemisphere, or half-brain, controls the right half of the body and is also the part of the brain that usually controls language and general cognitive functions. Lesions to this half of the brain can cause aphasia, which means that depending on where in the left brain the lesion occurs, a person will suffer from an inability to understand language or to produce speech or both. It is a nasty type of brain damage.

The right cortex, or hemisphere, or half-brain, does not normally contribute to language processes in any major way. It usually manages nonverbal processes, such as attention and subtle pattern discrimination like facial recognition and line orientation, and in the auditory domain such things as detecting the difference between complex tones.

Normally these two parts of the brain are interconnected through the corpus callosum. This single nerve fiber system constitutes the largest neural pathway in the animal kingdom. Its function, which was largely unknown until these studies, keeps each hemisphere aware of the activities of the other. As far as one can tell, it is a totally efficient reporting system, such that to discuss the normal intact person as left-brained or right-brained is nonsensical.

Our first chore was to determine whether or not Case W.J.'s brain was working normally according to the textbook guidelines. I started by testing the visual system. My lab in the Alles Building was a shell, not yet equipped with the usual paraphernalia of a biology lab. It did have one useful feature: exposed ceiling pipes. I built an enormous rear projection screen and hung it from these pipes. I then fitted slide projectors with mechanical shutters so that a picture could be quick-flashed to one or the other visual field. This meant each half-brain could be tested separately and we could also see whether information from each half-brain was communicated to the other in normal fashion.

Other tests were prepared that would test tactile function, that is, whether W.J. possessed normal sensory skills in his hands, legs, and face. It took a few months to sort it all out. When we were ready, Bogen brought W.J. up for his preoperative testing. The tests were uneventful. W.J. was entirely normal in his awareness of information presented to either hemisphere. His callosum was working perfectly. He returned home to await his surgery.

Bogen and his Professor of Neurosurgery, Peter Vogel, decided to cut the callosum and the anterior commissure in one operation. Their reasoning was the same as Van Wagenen's: they hoped the surgery would isolate any future seizures to one half-brain, keeping the other side seizure-free and in control so the patient would not suffer a generalized convulsion. When the other cases were done and after observing a few patients with an occasional postsurgical seizure, it became evident the mechanism of control was different. Instead of the patients having unilateral seizures at the same frequency as before their surgery, their seizure activity was vastly reduced overall. It was concluded that by cutting the callosum, the epileptogenic focus was more difficult to trigger, largely because of the tonic effects of having the callosum sectioned. Seizure control is obtained to a degree unknown before by the patients.

The first surgery was a success, although W.J., forty-eight years old at the time of the operation, took a long time to recover.[4] He remained in the hospital for about a month, and not until some time after that was he ready to come to Caltech for testing. It was a day charged with excitement for me. It turned out to be the beginning of a new era in human neuropsychology.

Bogen met me at the entrance in his resident's Good-Humorman garb, which I always kidded him about, and W.J. and his wife drove up from Downey. We helped him out of the car and placed him in his wheelchair. At Bogen's insistence W.J. wore a crash helmet in case he fell. W.J. was smiling and chipper. As we rolled him into the building, I remember receiving an incredulous glance from Max Delbruck who was walking back to his lab from lunch: somebody was going to learn something from this epileptic? (Delbruck was a biophysicist and a future Nobel laureate who many claim was one of the main guiding energies behind molecular biology.) We pressed on.

One of the most compelling features of split-brain surgery is the fact that the patient's behavior, affect, and general personality are totally untouched. Having the left brain disconnected from the right does not produce disturbances in everyday life, and the untrained eye would find it difficult to detail that a patient had had surgery at all. The dramatic effects can be observed only under careful laboratory conditions using the same procedures as our preoperative testing.

Let me explain it once again because it is difficult to keep straight. In the visual system if a person fixates a point in space, such as a dot on the wall, everything to the left of the dot is projected to the right half-brain's visual system and everything to the right of the dot is projected to the left half-brain. In the normal brain it doesn't make much difference where the information falls in the visual cortex because the connecting pathways between the two half-brains are intact. Information falling into the right visual field is directly projected to the left, speaking hemisphere. Information falling into the left visual field projects initially to the right brain but is then instantly communicated to the left hemisphere, which is normally dominant for language and speech. In the split-brain patient, this is not the case.

What we discovered that afternoon was the beginning of the split-brain story for humans. W.J.'s responses were completely different from his preoperative results. We rolled him into the room where my cinemascope-size projection screen was still dangling from the ceiling, and I turned on the shuttered slide projectors. I told W.J. to fixate the dot and proceeded to flash simple figures such as triangles, circles, and simple words. They were randomly arranged so it was not known which visual field and therefore which hemisphere would be exposed to the stimulus.

The results were clear. W.J. easily named the visual stimuli flashed into the right visual field; that is, to the left, speaking hemisphere. That half-brain performed just as well as it had before the surgery. When stimuli were flashed to the left visual field, however, W.J. said nothing after each trial. When questioned, he denied seeing the stimuli. The right hemisphere, now disconnected, had no way of transferring information to the left, which would engender a spoken response. It had become an independent mental system. The next challenge would be to determine what the isolated right brain could do.

Splitting the brain did make a difference in how information was shuttled around inside the head. The brain is not an amorphous system where any information can get to any point even in the presence of brain damage. W.J., while blindfolded, could easily name objects held in his right hand. When the same object was held in his left hand he could not name it. Touch is a different modality, but the disconnection is the same. Touch information from the right hand is normally cross-projected to the left brain. Since the left brain has speech and language, there was no problem in naming objects. But touch information for the left hand is cross-projected to the right brain which was now isolated. We were dazzled.

That was the first day of what was almost a weekly event for the next five years. There was consistency with the animal story and the way was now paved to try to figure out how each half-brain works in isolation. That work is still progressing, but much was accomplished during those first five years.

Most of the testing went on at W.J.'s home in Downey, since it was difficult for him to get to Caltech. I made a portable set of testing equipment and trooped down to his house in my old Studebaker. He and his wife always greeted me warmly. When he came to Caltech for testing it was usually on a Saturday or Sunday morning, and Sperry and I would test him together. After either type of session Sperry and I would talk in his office for a couple of hours about the meaning of what we had done. After my car trips to Downey, Sperry would take copious notes as I reported on the results of the day's testing. Those were glorious meetings. Sperry has a real skill for eliciting one's thoughts. He would let the conversation roam and not constrain the flow at all. His role here was essential and powerful. From these talks we developed the context and the framework that has now become the standard for this research. Our results were clearly reported, not encoded in incomprehensible medical jargon, since writing was another of Sperry's many talents.

W.J. was a bright man with a wry sense of humor. The object of one set of tests was to see whether or not his right hemisphere would respond to the sudden introduction of a pinup girl presented unexpectedly as one slide among more boring stimuli such as pictures of apples or spoons. W.J. sat there stoically after seeing the girl, saying he didn't see anything and with no change in his emotions. Disappointed, I packed my gear and headed back to Caltech. About halfway there I realized I hadn't tested his left hemisphere. I turned around and went back, set up my gear, ran through the whole thing, this time with the surprise coming into the left, talking hemisphere. Again, nothing with any emotion. Just something to the effect it had been a girl. I realized the stimuli weren't doing the trick and I was preparing to leave again when W.J. said, "Say, Mike, is that the kind of coed you have at Caltech?"

It wasn't all smooth going, however. The old saying that nothing is simpler than yesterday's solutions is one of the practical truisms in science. For everything that worked, there were twenty attempts that misfired. My favorite involved renting a penny arcade driving game and having it delivered to W.J.'s house. I thought I could use the device to learn about possible problems in visual-motor coordination. The purchasing agent at Caltech was incredulous. He wanted to know what I thought he was running. I told him to just do it, which he kindly did. The huge contraption arrived at W.J.'s and was set up on the patio. I sat down and played with it for a while and, pleased that I didn't have to put in my own quarters, I looked at the monster and asked myself, "Okay, big shot, what's the question? And, if you figure that out, what's the control?" I let W.J. play with it too and then ordered that it be picked up. I don't remember talking long with Roger about this episode.

The testing of W.J. went on for years and during that time we studied a variety of issues that dealt with problems in memory, language, attention, and motor control. The upshot of these first efforts was that the animal work was confirmed in man—the cutting of the cerebral commissures produced two separate mental systems, each with its own capacity to learn, remember, feel emotion, and behave. The notion that man is an indivisible conscious agent became questionable. The modern series of tests was launched. And W.J. was living happily in Downey, California, with no sense of the importance of the discoveries that had been made through observation of his behavior.

What is construed as an advance in knowledge often turns out to be corrective information, or information contradicting some common assumption or way of thinking. Such findings receive much attention because by their very nature they are counterintuitive. Our first studies had this quality. I can remember telling a psychologist one night about our findings. This person had spent a lifetime trying to figure out the psychological laws of reasoning. After I finished, he said, "So big deal. Now instead of trying to figure out one mind, you give me two. This is an advance?" The basic truth of his remark was enough to keep me busy in subsequent years as I tried to bring split-brain work into a paradigmatic setting that would illuminate the nature of human cognition. My chance to delve into the mechanisms of conscious experience would come after I left Caltech. Still, at the time, the finding of two independent minds in one brain was riveting because of its bearing on the common assumption of mental unity.

A few years into our work, Sperry was invited to a meeting at the Vatican that was being chaired by Sir John Eccles, a devout Catholic. Many of the leaders of brain research were there, and it was really the first major meeting at which Sperry would present our findings on the first two split-brain cases, W.J. and N.G.[5] In his typical fashion he played down the meeting. I, on the other hand, thought his studied nonchalance was in for trouble, not from the brain scientists, but from the papal scholars within the Vatican. As a good Catholic boy, I knew that they really knew. I couldn't wait for his return to hear about this historic meeting.

Sperry enjoys reducing puffery more than anyone I know. He also has a long-standing curiosity about how any intelligent person can take religion seriously. These views came together in his account of the meeting. With an outlandish eagerness I asked how it went. "Oh, the Vatican is a good place to take Kodacolors. All those priests running around in those brightly colored robes create quite a picture. The pope was kind of interesting. In his opening remarks he said we could have the brain so long as we left the mind to him." I was speechless at the time but have subsequently learned the pope didn't really say that. It was Sperry's way, I guess, of introducing me to the view that assumptions such as mine about the nature of man were based on a parochial set of Catholic assertions that had no value for working scientists—especially for the kind who spend their lives studying the nature of conscious experience.

But how were the original split-brain findings of "two minds in one brain" going to be followed up? The decision was to argue that the left and right half-brains are not only separate and distinct mental entities, each possessing different specialized skills, but that they also have distinctive cognitive styles. Thus began the most popularized versions of split-brain research. The second claim has been largely promoted by journalists or other scientists who have never examined a split-brain patient. Most of what they say is nonsense, but it is worth pondering in some detail.

CHAPTER 4

Left-Brain, Right-Brain Mania: A Debunking

OUT IN CALIFORNIA, left-brain/right-brain stories are a way of life. These stories all derive from the popularly held belief, supported by brain research, that the right brain is the place where our creative and synthetic impulses arise. There is a further belief that the right brain has been the black sheep of our educational and cultural system and that it is high time it received special attention. Thus the California state legislature is currently entertaining proposals for elementary school curricula that emphasize right-brain learning. Our schools are too cognitively rigid, so their story goes. We need more art courses to strengthen the right brain and allow us to become more creative.

This kind of thinking also makes its way into the media. An advertisement in a recent edition of *Esquire* magazine describes a machine that harmonizes the electrical patterns of each half-brain. For a mere eight thousand dollars, the user is assured he can feel more relaxed. The manufacturers tell us that the device grew out of our knowledge of brain function that emerged from the great discoveries of the 1960s and 1970s.

Or consider the 1984 Olympics. During the marathon an ABC reporter informed us that running helps build up the right side of the brain! With elaborate graphics, the report rambled on about jogging in the context of popular myths about the two sides of the brain.

Where does all of this conjecture come from? How did some laboratory findings of limited generality get so outrageously misinterpreted? Why were they picked up so hungrily by the press and then embraced by every sort of scientific dilettante? There are several reasons. The left-brain/right-brain dichotomy was simple and understandable and provided a way to talk about modern brain research and how it applied to everyday experience. Certainly no one was going to argue that people have artistic-intuitive skills and logical-linguistic skills. Prima facie there are manifestly different activities of mind. So science is used to prove that one set of skills is in the left brain and another in the right, which in turn proves that mental skills are different, and therefore able to be differentially trained. The image of one part of the brain doing one thing and the other part something entirely different was there, and that it was a confused concept seemed to make no difference.

Others like Robert Ornstein, a talented psychologist and clever popularizer, understood this and saw how the metaphor could be stretched to include modes of thought as they existed in contemporary culture. He put together a highly successful book drawing upon Eastern and Western cultists, brain scientists, and other psychologists.[1] Left-brain and right-brain cognitive styles became shorthand for a hundred different views of styles of life that ranged from the ridiculous to the absurd. Yet each appealed to someone. Indeed, when this shorthand becomes a cartoon in *The New Yorker* (see frontispiece), you know it has become a part of the culture.

The runaway fervor for such ideas relates, in part, to the difficulty in communicating scientific ideas to the general public. To really understand concepts arising out of experimental data is a serious business, and most people do not have the time or interest to assess information at that level. There is an extensive and usually foreign vocabulary to learn. The necessary qualifying remarks and constraints on the ideas prove to be too much of a burden for the potential audience. So scientific journalism purveys its stories on simple-to-understand claims that most people can relate to, preferably at a personal level. This wouldn't matter for the present story except for the fact that the distortions get in the way of why split-brain patients are truly interesting. And, the oversimplifications and outright erroneous information have also tended to trivialize the complexity of the integrated processes of our minds.

Let me go back to the research related to this issue and try to explain what the studies do mean and what they do not mean. I'll start with Case W.J. since he was the first to show interesting asymmetries in what is called a visual-spatial task.[2]

It all started on a sunny afternoon in Downey, California, in 1961. W.J. was shown a picture of a cube and then asked to draw it. His left hand had no problem with the task; his right hand was completely unable to accomplish it (see figure 4.1). The same sort of thing proved to be true for a test called Kohs Blocks.[3] This test consists of a standard set of red-and-white blocks and requires the person being tested to arrange them to match a picture design. Again, his right hand could not perform the task but the left one could. This was consistent with the general neurologic literature on focal left- or right-brain damage. What had never been observed before was the presence of a function in one half-brain along with its absence from the other. It was a startling sight and I immediately wanted to have it filmed.

Caltech bought me an old Bolex, and I asked my friend Baron Wolmon, a consummate photographer, to take the pictures at W.J.'s house. They were beautiful and had a significant impact. I placed a simple pattern on a card in full view on a white tablecloth on W.J.'s favorite coffee table. Wolmon fixed the lights and the Bolex and I then placed next to the pattern the four blocks that had to be arranged to match the pattern. I let W.J.'s left hand go first, the one that gets its major control from

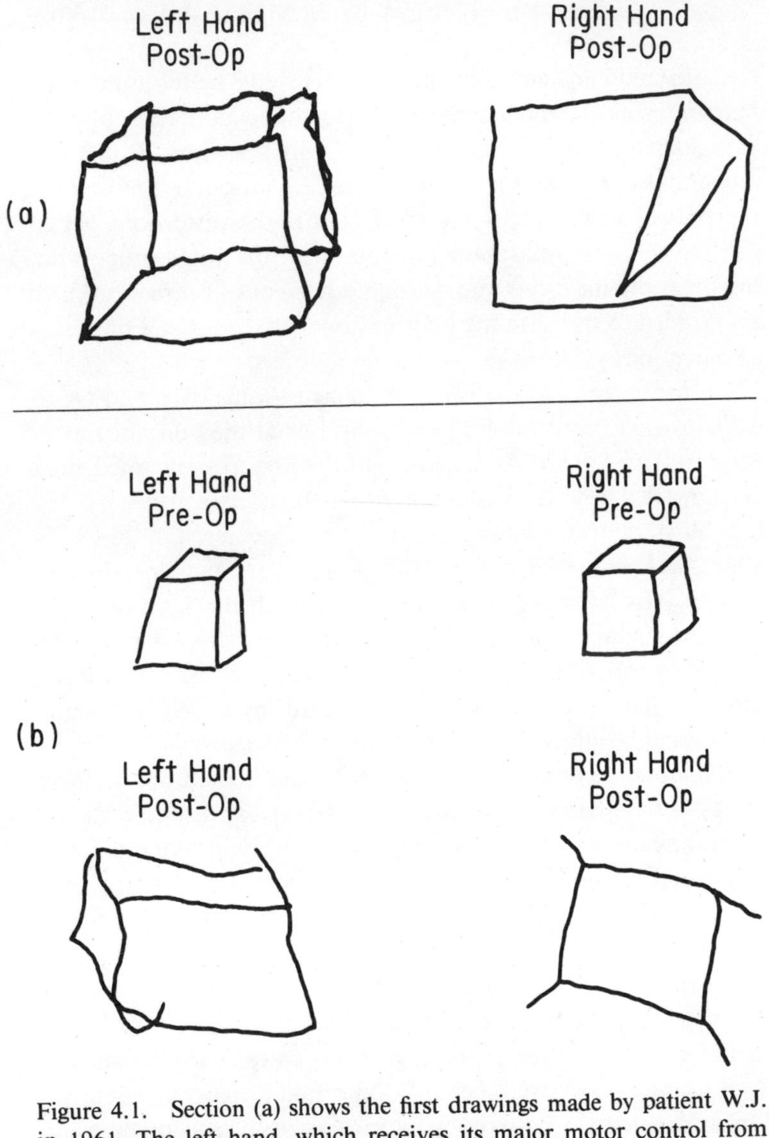

Figure 4.1. Section (a) shows the first drawings made by patient W.J. in 1961. The left hand, which receives its major motor control from the right hemisphere, was able to carry out the task with greater skill than the right hand. The right, which receives its major control from the left hemisphere, the dominant language center, performs poorly. Section (b) shows the results of testing patient P.S., who was studied years later at Cornell Medical Center.

the right brain. Swiftly and easily the blocks were correctly arranged. I then picked the blocks up, mixed them up, and placed them back on the table. W.J.'s task was now to do the same chore with his dominant right hand. This hand receives its major innervation from the left, talking brain. We ran out of film as we watched him struggle with the task. At several instances during the filming, the left hand tried to intervene and help the incompetent right hand. That side of his brain-body knew how to do this task. His failure was riveting and completely convincing.

Wolmon reloaded the camera and this time I told W.J. he could use either hand. It was the first time I saw how the two mental systems could get into a struggle of major proportions. The left hand would make progress at solving the task and then the right would come in and undo the left's superior accomplishments. It was as if they were in a duel, and this observation led to the design of many other experiments that I will discuss later.

Still, the major observation was the dissociation of competencies between the two half-brains. The claim that we based on those findings was that the left brain was dominant for language processes and the right brain was dominant for visual-constructional tasks. In subsequent years this concept underwent radical revision based on a new set of experiments by others, and it emerged in a barely recognizable form. It is the interpretation of these new experiments that made me part company with my mentor and his new colleagues. Their views struck me as implausible. For example, Jerre Levy and Roger Sperry took a different tack and in published reports claimed that the right brain was specialized for holistic processes and the left was necessary for analytical processes.[4] As they put it, "The data indicate that the mute, minor hemisphere is specialized for Gestalt perception, being primarily a synthesist in dealing with information input. The speaking (left) hemisphere, in contrast, seems to operate in a more logical, analytic, computer-like fashion. Its language is inadequate for the rapid complex synthesis achieved by the minor hemisphere." It was a provocative idea, yet based on extremely limited data. Bogen's interpretation of the same new experiments was more conservative. He did not favor characterizing the two sides in the usual dichotomies of verbal versus visual-spatial or analytic versus holistic. He preferred the terms "appositional versus propositional" by which he meant the right brain takes in stimuli and apposes or compares them to prior information. It behaves in a more automatic and direct way.

Nonetheless, Levy, Bogen, Trevarthen, and Sperry were convinced the differences between the right and left brains were real and were to be understood in the way they dealt with information. In considering whether or not to accept the veracity of such conclusionary views, it is helpful to consider the experiments that gave rise to the ideas.

The key experiment used what are called chimeric figures.[5] They were things like two half-faces stuck together to make a whole face, but with the left half being a picture of person A and the right half being a picture of person B. Split-brain subjects were then asked to fixate a dot on a screen and the chimeric picture was flashed. Thus, the left brain saw the right half-face of person B and the right brain saw the left half-face of person A. After presentation of the stimulus, the subject was required to choose from a set of faces the one it had seen. The choices were all normal full-face pictures of the half-faces.

The results showed that the faces presented to the right brain were more often responded to than those presented to the left. This was easily detected by simply observing which picture the subject chose after each trial. It was also reported, informally, that the left brain of the split-brain subjects had a hard time learning the names of the faces presented in the experiment. This, it was suggested, was due to the fact that the gestalt analyzer that was active for such stimulus processing was in the right brain, and the naming mechanism, which was in the left, could not coordinate the two respective skills. It was also noted that when the left brains of these subjects were asked to describe the faces the subjects always commented on specific features such as whether or not the head was bald, had a mustache, or wore glasses. This was thought to demonstrate the analytic nature of the left brain as compared to the holistic analysis given by the right brain.

There are, however, a number of other possible interpretations of this kind of experiment. That the subjects favored the right-brain stimuli does not necessarily mean that the right brain was responding more assertively because of a specialized gestalt analyzer. The reason could be that it asserts itself simply because it is able to respond to such stimuli since it is by definition a system of markedly limited capacities. The left, in considering more aspects of such stimuli, merely loses out to the more literal direct system of the right brain.

Second, the observation that the subjects had difficulty learning names for faces, an observation that received more attention than the primary findings, is totally meaningless. The rate of learning names for the faces for the left brains was compared to the rate at which Caltech undergraduates learned to associate a name with a picture. That, as they say, is comparing apples and oranges.

Finally, the observation that the left brain's description of the faces demonstrated it was analytic as opposed to gestalt in nature is also without meaning. How else is a talking brain supposed to describe a face except to describe its obvious features?

With all the leeway for contrasting interpretations of the data, more experiments needed to be carried out. The experiments had raised interesting questions and after a few years it became clear such studies were the backbone for the larger, more irresponsible claims about left and right brains. The first studies were done by Joseph LeDoux and myself.[6]

We first made sure our patients displayed the same basic

phenomena such as was in Case W.J. Figure 4.1 shows a drawing by Case P.S., an attempt to draw a cube with his right hand as opposed to the more able left hand. At the level of analysis given our first Case W.J., it could be said we had come across confirmatory findings. The left hand, which receives its major motor control from the right brain which is specialized for such tasks, is better able to draw than is the right hand which receives its major control from the left or language brain. But what does it mean? Is the left/right difference in the execution of the task, or in the perception of the task, or both? Is it true for everybody? Are all right brains superior at such tasks or are only some?

When Sperry, Bogen, and I first reported this data, it was our thought that the difference was more in the execution of the task.[7] There was something special about the right brain's ability to take a visual image and to instruct the motor system of the brain on how to draw the matching figure or arrange the blocks to match the diagram. The right brain had some sensory-motor coupling capacity the left didn't have. It was not, we felt, that the right brain was superior at perceiving the objects themselves.

At the time we said all of that, we hadn't done the key experiments to back up the claim. It just seemed logical. Years later LeDoux and I working on the Dartmouth patients did the proper studies and the work basically confirmed the notion that the right brain was specialized for something in the executive realm but was not superior at the simple apprehension of visual stimuli. The studies were simple enough. Instead of asking the patient to arrange blocks to match the stimulus, we merely asked if the patient could match the stimulus to another set of pictures. In other words, no manipulation of the blocks was required. The task was simple picture-to-picture match.[8] Under these conditions the differences between the two brains disappeared. As a result it was reasoned that when a task involved manipulating objects with the left hand, the right brain seemed superior. That distinction still holds in all patients.

Nonetheless, we were now set to test the chimeric stimulus

story. We generated a series of stimuli that mimicked the chimeric stimuli used in the earlier experiments. We reran the basic experiment first on Case P.S., whom I will describe in detail shortly. We were able to run the experiment on him very soon after his split-brain surgery. This is important. In the Levy study, the patients all had undergone their surgery a number of years before her tests.

Case P.S. was instantly able to point to both stimuli, the right half-picture flashed to the left brain and the left half-picture flashed to the right. In his early postoperative days there was no favoring of one brain over the other. What is extremely interesting, however, is that when the tests were rerun after the first post-operative year, the right brain became more assertive on such tests and made most of the responses. The same result has now been found on a number of other patients. Why?

Why is it in a family that more often than not one person will make breakfast and his or her mate will make dinner? It is impractical that both do both jobs even though both are capable. There is often only one stove. As a result a behavioral resolution is adopted. One person will perform one task and one person will perform the other. So too with a left brain and a right brain working within the same cranium. In the nervous system there is what is called the "final common path," a concept that refers to the group of neurons that exit from the brain to innervate the arms or legs. Matching pictures of shapes and faces and the like is something the right brain can do. As a rule it cannot talk. Thus a tacit agreement is reached. The left brain does the talking, the right brain does the simpler matching tasks. This kind of behavioral resolution can mislead one to think hemispheric modes of thinking or specialization are being observed when in fact they are not.

As for the generality of the informal observation that the split-brain subjects had a hard time learning names for the faces, that too proved to be most likely a spurious observation. In tests explicitly run to see whether or not one brain had more difficulty learning a name for a face, the left brain proved as facile as the right. This test, of course, used facial stimuli that were sufficiently dissimilar such that each half-brain could easily tell them apart.

Still there have been persistent reports that patients with right-sided lesions were terrible at remembering normal faces that looked more similar than not. In a set of studies by Robin Yin at M.I.T., for example, stimuli were used that were not confounded by having some heads have glasses or mustaches or the like that made them easily identifiable with a verbal code.[9] We reasoned that if those findings were true, the disconnected right brain should be excellent at detecting such faces and the disconnected left should perform poorly. We went back to the testing lab and tested our patients on this task. The patients were V.P. and P.S., two who can talk out of the left brain and right brain, and J.W. who could talk only out of the left brain.[10]

In each test a face is presented to the left brain and the patient is required to select the match from a series of ten faces. In all patients the left brain performed the task poorly. The right brain, however, found the task simple and performed well. This situation persists for years after surgery, even in patients whose right brains have shown plasticity in developing speech. The right-brain plasticity given over to this enterprise does not seem present for facial perception in the left brain. This study appears to support the idea that there is in the right brain a specialized system for controlling this kind of stimulus processing. In further studies it appeared the special skill is not for faces per se, but for stimuli that go beyond the ability of a verbal system to describe their nature. Thus studies on distinguishing subtle line orientations also showed a right-hemisphere effect.

Other tests have been designed by other investigators studying the same California patients. One of the tests that was particularly intriguing was carried out by Robert Nebes.[11] He had the patient hold in one hand a cutout geometric shape such as a triangle. If the object was held in the left hand, the right brain was processing the information; if held in the right hand, the left brain was processing the information. He then had the patient point to one of three pictures, each an exploded line drawing of a geometric shape, one an exploded figure of the triangle. The task was to point to the correct exploded figure. Nebes found that the left hand performed the task much better than the right. He and others concluded this indicated the right brain was superior at apprehending visual information since it seemed able to synthesize the figural elements with greater efficiency.

There are a number of problems with such interpretations. To set the stage for proper criticism let me describe one more experiment, this one carried out by Dr. Brenda Milner and her colleague Laughlin Taylor of the Montreal Neurological Institute.[12] They studied the same patients and unearthed the fact that the left hand was able to retrieve nonsense tactile shapes with much greater accuracy than was the right. The shapes were irregularly shaped wire figures that the subject had to feel with the hand and, subsequent to that, find the exact same object from a set of four others. This simple match-to-sample test carried out within the touch modality was quickly done with the left hand, but not with the dominant right hand. Thus a natural bias in the brain enables the left hand to process hard-to-verbalize touch information better than the right hand does.

We have reproduced these findings in some of our patients. The built-in bias for processing nonverbal tactile information seems to be a real, superior property of the right brain. What LeDoux and I also showed was that the asymmetry was not in the perceptual apprehension per se. Thus, if the entire test was presented within the visual modality, no asymmetries were seen. That is, if a picture of one of the irregular wire figures was presented to the left or right brain, either hemisphere could point to which of the wire figures it was.

It began to look more and more as if there was something specific about using the left hand to obtain some results suggesting perceptual asymmetries. In this light we reexamined the Nebes study on the exploded figures. Sure enough, if a picture of one of the geometric shapes was presented to one or the other half-brain, either one could easily point to which exploded figure depicted the visually presented shape. Yet, when the opposite was done, the phenomenon returned. That is, when a picture of one of the exploded figures was flashed to the right brain and the left hand, the use of touch could find the answer with ease. Flashing the picture to the left brain found the right hand performing poorly. At least that is how our results came out in some patients. And in some cases we do not find the asymmetry at all, under any conditions.

Then there is the other problem. Do all patients show the same kind of left/right asymmetry for these kinds of tasks? Consider this about J.W. He loves cars and quite clearly is a talented artist. Pre-operationally he drew dozens of pictures of cars with his right hand since he is normally right-handed. Current cant about left-brain and right-brain processes would say that prior to his surgery such processes were actually being mediated by the right brain and that the callosum sent the information over to the left where it was used to guide the right hand's response. After full split-brain surgery, there are no differences in the quality of the drawings. Both sets of pictures are superb, yet the second set was drawn at a time when we know J.W. could not accurately guide the right hand from the right hemisphere. The drawing was completely engineered from the left brain. (J.W. also draws nice cubes with either hand.)

Quite simply, all brains are not organized the same way. Special talents like those seen in J.W. can reside in the right brain or in the left. Clearly what is important is not so much where things are located, but that specific brain systems handle specific tasks. We begin to see that the brain has a modular nature, a point that comes out of all of the data. It is of only secondary interest that the modules should always be in the same place. A correlate of this is that much of split-brain research should be viewed as a technique to expose modularity. That is, it is not important that the left brain does this or the right brain does that. But it is highly interesting that by studying patients with their cerebral hemispheres separated certain mental skills can be observed in isolation. It is a hugely significant point.

Clearly, therefore, one can detect asymmetries in the processing of information. It can be a very robust, or striking, phenomenon, but it is without a doubt one of the most elusive to accurately characterize. Some half-brains exhibit the asymmetry and some don't. Some studies suggest it is perceptual in nature, and some suggest it is tied to a more manual response. Still others, such as I, wonder whether it is not more apparent than real. To use a computer metaphor, do these asymmetries reflect a software difference or a more structurally based hardware difference between the two brains? Consider the following.

Instead of thinking of the right brain as possessing a specialized module for the processing of such information, it could be that the left brain, under stimulus conditions that find its natural disposition to codify a stimulus frustrated, allocates more resources to such an attempt and thereby focuses less on the simple task of attending to the key features of the stimulus that would allow for a subsequent perceptual match. The right hemisphere, which does not have such a rich hypothesis-generating apparatus, allocates all of its resources to the simple task at hand and, as a result, relative to the left brain, scores higher on the memory-loaded perceptual task. Such an interpretation of the phenomenon cannot be ruled out at present. In fact, at this time I prefer it to all others since it can explain almost all left/right data.

By the late 1960s and early 1970s the realization was spreading that the simple dichotomies of that time did little to advance knowledge about how cognitive systems work. Neuropsychology was at risk. Isolating mental systems or claiming that isolated mental systems process information differently does not really illuminate the nature of cognition. This realization was responsible for much of the new work that started with the East Coast series of patients.

CHAPTER 5

Brain Mechanisms and Belief Formation

MOST PEOPLE in science do not stay fixed to one problem. It seems that way from the outside because most people do wind up discovering they are interested in particular kinds of problems and those are the ones they write about. Yet, within a typical scientific career, there is the normal amount of boredom that comes from working on any problem for a long period; when that happens breaks are taken and other interests are tried on for size. Something is gained from these experiences but usually the mind returns to its original interests. I was to return to human split-brain research, but I would take a wholly different approach from the one we had developed at Caltech. The new studies would eventually provide insights into how we humans form beliefs. But as I say, I first played with other ideas.

I left California in 1969 bound for the rigors of East Coast life. After leaving Caltech in 1966 I spent a few months in Pisa with my good friend, Giovanni Berlucchi. Disciplined, highly intelligent, and dedicated, Berlucchi tried his best to turn me into a neurophysiologist. Our mission was nothing short of trying to crack the brain code. When he had visited Caltech for a year, Berlucchi had become interested, as I was, in the corpus callosum. Since we knew that severing the structure eliminated the transfer of learning and memory between the two brains, we decided to study the response of single cells in this "mind cable" and see if we could understand how it worked. Our efforts were to lead to some of the first single-cell recordings of the callosum, not only in Italy, but in the world. Berlucchi and his colleague, Giacomo Rizzolatti, continued their electrophysiological work, which became a cornerstone in the analysis of visual processes that are transmitted between the two half brains.

It was an invigorating experience for me, and watching my Italian colleagues setting up the new technology of single-cell recording in a garden laboratory in Pisa was a pleasure. The Italians work with single purpose. Nothing stops them once they set their minds to a task, even though there are moments of hilarity along the way.

One afternoon after weeks of preparing the laboratory, all was ready for recording from the callosum. The bank of complex electrophysiological equipment was ready; amplifiers were tuned up to record the first nerve cell crossing between the two half-brains of a cat. The cat was immobile, looking ahead at a screen where visual stimuli would be presented and the expected neural response recorded. The microelectrode was just above the callosum and about to be lowered into the structure that was going to be crucial to the brain code. About fifteen expectant scientists crowded into the little recording room.

Rizzolatti lowered the electrode into the callosum. Just as the electrode hit the callosum an electrical ground loop closed and, instead of hearing the popping, static-like sound of a neuron, the sounds of the Beatles singing "We all live in a yellow submarine" burst forth over the loudspeaker. Rizzolatti looked up, cocked his glasses forward, and said, "This is high-order information?"

I left Italy and all of this to return to the University of California at Santa Barbara. It was a period of transition. While I returned to a fully funded grant to continue my split-brain work on both animals and humans, I was told that my efforts on the human subjects were not appreciated by the Caltech group. Whereas all of my plans to study the patients at Santa

Barbara had been pre-approved at Caltech before I moved, things changed in predictable ways. I was annoyed at first, but then let it pass, as I had become disappointed in Santa Barbara. It was a beautiful but sleepy place. Leon Festinger, at that time a new acquaintance, had just moved to New York from Stanford. We had met at a seminar I gave at Stanford and quickly became fast friends. Festinger, after establishing the field of modern social psychology, switched his interest to visual perception. He called from the New School in New York, where he had taken a position. "N.Y.U. wants a physiological psychologist. Do you want the job?" And after a little negotiating and at least twenty-three changes of mind, I took it.

Californians arriving in New York City have to be among the most trying groups of people in the world. All they talk about is the easy life and the good weather back home. They can be insufferable, and I was among their number until New York took hold. The people, then the restaurants invade your thoughts. The excellent faculty at N.Y.U. were very supportive. People there were interested in more things and the pace of extracurricular information was swift. In addition there was Festinger who is a walking university. Every week we had lunch and talked about everything from eyeballs to social structure. Living in an intensely social place like New York makes one more acutely aware of the social dimensions of work. New York living invades everything.

In addition to my studies on humans I had always carried out extensive experimental studies on animals. In experiments with animals, ideas developed in work with patients could be followed up in more detail and with greater control. Upon arriving in New York I was quick to set up my monkey lab. Several students had come with me from Santa Barbara and they worked hard to get things going fast. On the clinical end my connections with hospitals were sort of hit-and-miss. Hans-Lukas Teuber, then the charismatic head of the M.I.T. psychology department, had generously introduced me to the head of neurology at

N.Y.U. Medical Center. I went over to see the chairman, who happened to be housed in what had been Teuber's space at N.Y.U. before he moved to Boston. I wanted to start a new project with neurologic patients suffering from language disorders, and that seemed like the logical place. The chairman greeted me with a superior medical air and said, "You see these labs. These used to be Teuber's neuropsychology labs. I personally think neuropsychology is a bunch of bullshit. Now what is it you want to do?" I mumbled something about the importance of the brain in understanding behavior and departed his office with a certain relief. With a little work I found another niche, far more pleasant, through N.Y.U.'s Rehabilitation Hospital.

But I missed human split-brain research. I knew the problems and issues, and I could read the continuing papers with a critical eye since the studies were all being carried out on patients I had first characterized. I knew the story line coming out in the early 1970s from Caltech was full of problems and limitations, but I had no way to verify and support my own views.

Then I was asked by Dartmouth College Medical School to come up and give a talk. I looked forward to that with great pleasure. It was returning home, but from the other side of the desk. After my lecture, a neurosurgeon named Donald Wilson approached me and, to my amazement, asked if I would be interested in testing some of his split-brain patients. I couldn't believe my ears. Wilson had been carrying out the procedure for about two years and had several patients, none of whom had been studied by an experimental neuropsychologist. I jumped at the opportunity and ever since then I have had an active association with Dartmouth.

The series of patients my colleagues and I now test come from several different medical centers in the East. But before I discuss the patients, let me say a word about the people who are part of the medical and scientific aspects of this work. Dr. Donald Wilson of Dartmouth is credited for developing the surgery to its present fine form. He vigorously took part in all medical aspects of the research and supported our efforts throughout. Dr. Wilson died in 1982, and all who worked with him will miss him enormously. He was a true gentleman. I am happy to say his protégé, Dr. David Roberts, continues to deliver these much-needed medical skills to the New England community. In addition to doing work at the Dartmouth-Mary Hitchcock Clinic, my colleagues and I also study a patient from the Medical College of Ohio where Dr. Mark Rayport heads a program in the surgical control of epilepsy. Dr. Rayport started his series, largely inspired by Dr. Wilson's success, a few years back. He is a senior surgeon and enjoys a superior reputation for his surgical skills. We also study patients from Yale and the University of Minnesota.

Since 1972 I have worked in collaboration with a series of talented graduate students and postdoctoral research fellows. The first studies were largely done with Joseph LeDoux, Gail Risse, and Pamela Greenwood. We bought a used house trailer, converted it into a mobile lab, and for four years dragged it behind a van for monthly trips up to New England. The wear and tear on us all somehow paled next to the excitement of going there and doing the work.

I left N.Y.U. in 1972 and accepted an attractive offer from the State University of New York at Stony Brook. At Stony Brook a group of new students tackled the problems of split-brain research with me. In 1977 I moved my laboratory from Stony Brook to Cornell Medical School in New York City. Moving back to New York City was exhilarating, and I buried myself in work. Joseph LeDoux, my student and a man of unrelenting generosity, came along with me before going out on his own. As a parting shot to split-brain research, LeDoux stuck an equipment request for a twenty-six-foot GMC motor home into a grant application to the National Science Foundation (NSF). Ironically, his budget justification for the van was sufficiently compelling that the NSF awarded the van but not the rest of the grant. According to reports that filtered back to us, the review panel caught the spirit of our trips, sort of like Steinbeck's *Travels with Charley.* Those not involved in a particular trip always look disappointed when the rest of us leave. The trips are usually scientific adventures, but they are always full of laughs and good times.

The current research staff is wonderful to work with. Until his sudden and tragic death, fast, facile, data-ingenious Jeffrey Holtzman, a student of Leon Festinger, kept us all laughing with his otherwise views of almost everything. Then there is seemingly sober, responsible, Columbia-educated John Sidtis, who sometimes has to be physically restrained from making demands for urban amenities on the hotels and restaurants of rural New England. Bruce Volpe, a neurologist and internist by training—had he gone into private practice he could be building his bookshelves of eighteen-karat gold instead of orange crates—has succumbed to the excitement of research and the experimental approach to the study of cognition. Finally there is my wife and colleague, Charlotte Smylie. Her sparkling, captivating ways not only enable her to usually ride herd on all of us (she's a Texan), but also to run half of the experiments when she isn't driving the van and listening to Emmylou Harris. We have a tradition of going on one of our New England trips each Thanksgiving, and every year Charlotte is somehow able to convert the mobile lab into a dining room and serve a four-course turkey dinner with candelabra (made out of aluminum foil). It is always the best trip of the year.

The first patients in our Dartmouth series were of limited interest. They basically confirmed the more neurological aspects of the California series. One hemisphere couldn't communicate with the other, the left brain talked but the right didn't, and so on. Then came Case P.S., the patient who opened a whole new way of looking at cerebral lateralization and the brain mechanisms involved in conscious experience. We have invested and continue to invest much time and effort in the understanding of Case P.S., as well as two similar cases, V.P. and J.W., which came

Figure 5.1. The inside of our trusty van with our gear and my not-so-reverent colleagues, John Sidtis and the late Jeff Holtzman.

along right after P.S. I will begin the story by telling you about these three extraordinary human beings.

P.S., a fifteen-year-old boy living in a trailer park in Vermont, suffers from epilepsy. The disease is a major concern in the hills of Vermont and New Hampshire, where it is common. P.S. had been referred to the Dartmouth Medical Center for help in controlling his seizures. Medications were not working, and a normal life did not appear possible.

Dr. Alexander Reeves, the talented neurologist in charge, first tried juggling the drugs, checking blood levels, and using all the other methods that are less invasive than brain surgery. Nothing worked. P.S. was a candidate for split-brain surgery. As usual, we were called and went to test P.S. preoperatively.

Dragging our own trailer behind us, we pulled into the trailer park. One forgets that people live in trailers, and in small, dull towns. I knocked on the door of a trailer and out flew this kid with nerve-racking energy whom we all grew to love. P.S. is an adolescent of low-average intelligence, with all of the conflicts and aspirations of a "normal" youth. He wants to be a computer programmer, an electrician, and a race car driver; he wants to move to Boston, to fall in love, and so on.

P.S. proved to be normal in every way according to our tests. Sensory information presented to either the left or the right visual field could be named easily. The same was true for touch information presented to either the left or right hand. Auditory information could not be tested because of a preexisting hearing loss in the right ear.

P.S. was operated on in January 1975. He proved to be a most extraordinary patient, at once confirming the earlier California studies and showing us that the split-brain story was far richer than we had previously imagined.[1] We tested him within a month after his full callosal surgery. He was unique. All the usual abilities were present, such as lateral specialization for drawing cubes, arranging blocks, and other right-hemisphere skills; and while his left hemisphere could talk normally about its experiences, it could not talk about experiences going on in the right half-brain. That was nothing new to me. The new finding from this series of patients was that P.S., like two of the fifteen California patients I had originally studied, could understand language in the right hemisphere. This is not normally the case.

A traditional test for right-hemisphere language is to flash words to the left visual field. The patient typically states that he doesn't see anything (this is the left hemisphere talking), and the test is seemingly over. However, if P.S.'s hand was placed underneath a table where several objects were laid out, after palpating the various selections he would pick up the appropriate object, the one whose name was flashed to the left visual field. His right hemisphere understood the meaning of nouns, just as those of the two California cases had.

Yet unlike the previous patients, P.S. could carry out commands presented to the right half-brain. If we flashed the verb, "smile," he would smile. If we flashed the word, "tap," he would tap the table in front of him. His right hemisphere could respond to verbal commands. This ability was unique at the time, and predicted a vast number of interesting features of the syndrome that I will be discussing.

Case V.P. came to us from Ohio. Dr. Rayport called to ask if we would be interested in studying her. Of course we were and we flew her to New York. By the time we saw her she had already undergone surgery. In her case it was carried out in two stages, with the anterior half of the callosum sectioned approximately ten weeks before the posterior half was sectioned. V.P. is a charming, socially alert, and dutiful young woman who works hard to please. She is divorced and lives with her young daughter. Like most of the patients, V.P. has parents who have an intense interest in her well-being and look after her with great care and concern.

We knew from the first visit that V.P. would be another special case. Like the others already mentioned, she initially displayed the full syndrome as classically described. Her right hemisphere was specialized for certain tasks and her left hemisphere could not talk about events transpiring in the right half-brain.[2]

That's where the similarity ends. Like P.S., she possessed an enormous amount of linguistic skill in her right half-brain. V.P. could also carry out commands. While initially she could not speak from her right brain, she could write out messages about information presented to her disconnected right brain. Our analysis of these phenomena follows the description of our last patient, J.W.

J.W. is another patient from the Dartmouth series. His epilepsy started later in life at age nineteen and caused serious social disruptions. He had been divorced twice and had been in continual trouble in his small New England town. His very caring parents finally took him to Dr. Wilson who, after a careful preoperative workup with Dr. Reeves, decided split-brain surgery was the only solution. As with so many of the other cases, the surgery proved stabilizing and helpful.

J.W. also had his surgery carried out in two stages. We were able to study him preoperatively, interoperatively, and postoperatively.[3] This opportunity led to some interesting observations about how information transfer between the two hemispheres takes place. J.W. resembled in psychological profile the two flagship California cases, L.B. and N.G., that I had first reported in my thesis; these two cases became the backbone of the California studies that continued after I left. J.W. provided a bridge between the two series and a chance for relevant comparisons. That is, J.W., like V.P. and P.S., could understand language in the right hemisphere but was not as proficient overall. Needless to say, he showed all the other standard split-brain effects.

These three patients are the subjects of most of our studies. There are many other split-brain patients but I will not discuss them here for a variety of reasons, the most important being that most split-brain patients do not possess right hemisphere language. Following surgery it is common to see the talking left hemisphere continuing its talkative ways. Information presented to the appropriate visual field or objects placed in the right hand are all named with normal facility. Yet unlike the cases of J.W., V.P., and P.S., information presented to the right half-brain yields nothing in response. The right half-brain has no language capacity and along with that a striking inactivity that borders on behavioral tedium. This is not to say these right hemispheres do not have specialized systems. They may have, but it is next to impossible to demonstrate their existence in a brain system that is so unable to behave overtly.

Cases like J.W., V.P., and P.S. are rare, and therefore raise the question of the wisdom of building a set of observations on a small minority of cases. I think it is not a problem because the studies to be reported are not of the traditional left-brain/right-brain variety that explore possible differences between the two sides. On that issue the split-brain data fall into the context of other clinical studies and studies on normals that do allow for such observations.

The approach I am taking here is different. I will describe how the left hemispheres of our three special patients deal with assertive behaviors produced by their right half-brains. By careful analysis of these phenomena, I hope to show how these insights give clues to the conscious processes in all of us.

Consider the everyday life of a split-brain patient. The dominant left hemisphere is dealing with the world, fielding its questions, planning action, accounting for the body's moods, and so on. Suddenly, the right half-brain decides it wants the patient to take a walk. What does the left brain do? What does it think? More generally, what does the left brain make of the activities initiated by the right half-brain?

These kinds of questions can be asked under strict laboratory conditions. Figure 5.2 depicts a typical experiment which LeDoux and I first carried out.[4] In brief, the experiment requires each

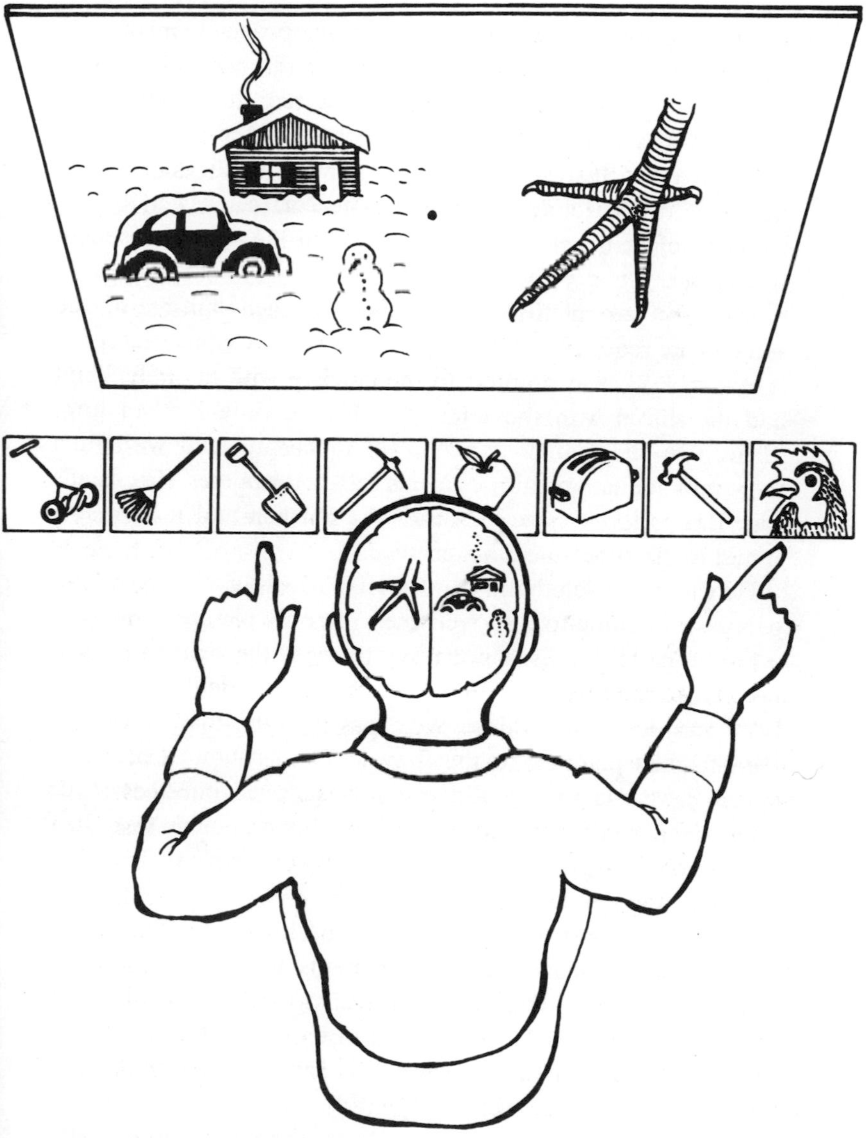

Figure 5.2. Two problems are presented simultaneously, one to the talking left brain and one to the nontalking right brain. The answers for each problem are available in full view in front of the patient.

SOURCE: Reprinted with permission from Michael S. Gazzaniga and Joseph LeDoux, *The Integrated Mind* (New York: Plenum, 1978).

hemisphere to solve a simple conceptual problem. A distinct picture is lateralized to one hemisphere: in this case the left sees a picture of a claw. At the same time the right hemisphere sees a picture of a snow scene. Placed in front of the patient are a series of cards that serve as possible answers to the implicit questions of what goes with what. The correct answer for the left hemisphere is a chicken. The answer for the right hemisphere is a shovel.

After the two pictures are flashed to each half-brain, the subjects are required to point to the answers. A typical response is that of P.S., who pointed to the chicken with his right hand and the shovel with the left. After his response I asked him, "Paul, why did you do that?" Paul looked up and without a moment's hesitation said from his left hemisphere, "Oh, that's easy. The chicken claw goes with the chicken and you need a shovel to clean out the chicken shed."

Here was the left half-brain having to explain why the left hand was pointing to a shovel when the only picture it saw was a claw. The left brain is not privy to what the right brain saw because of the brain disconnection. Yet the patient's very own body was doing something. Why was it doing that? Why was the left hand pointing to the shovel? The left-brain's cognitive system needed a theory and instantly supplied one that made sense given the information it had on this particular task. It is hard to describe the spell-binding power of seeing such things. Manipulating mind variables is awesome.

This basic observation has been made hundreds of times on these three patients. In the two patients who can respond to printed commands presented exclusively to the right hemisphere, it is simple to create the same kind of experimental conditions. A simple command such as "walk" is flashed to the mute right half-brain and the patient will typically respond by pushing his or her chair back and starting to leave the testing area. When asked where he or she is going, a typical response is "Going into my house to get a Coke." As before, the left hemisphere is faced with the task of explaining an overt behavior that was initiated not by that hemisphere but by the disconnected right half-brain. This phenomenon so clearly seen in the patients provides a major clue to conscious mechanisms, the system of rules that help normal people build up a personal sense of conscious awareness.

With time, and taking into account changing attitudes of each patient, the powerful and compelling phenomenon just described can take on many different forms. It is always there, but sometimes it has to be more subtly elicited. For example, there are times when Case J.W. might have temporarily adopted a philosophical view of matters in general and be urging the more or less reflexive attitude that he doesn't know why he does anything, especially if he is being constantly questioned by me. In such states of mind he might well offer at the end of each trial the clear response that he doesn't know why he pointed to one of the two objects because he doesn't know why he does anything, and so on.

When such a state of mind exists, we have merely to change our task to elicit the basic function of his left interpretive brain. We have to let his interpretive brain deal with a more subtle response. For example, we flash two words to J.W. One goes to the silent right brain and one to the talkative left brain. We ask J.W. to draw with his right hand a picture of what he sees. In one example J.W. was presented with the word "fire" to the right brain and "house" to the left. We sat back and videotaped the response.

First he drew a houselike structure, which was consonant with the left-brain stimulus. Then he began to draw crossroads to show the house in a key location in a town, the location of the firehouse. When he put his pen down, we asked what it was he had drawn. Startled, he picked up the pen, made some more scratches, and said, "A tree house." He then added some marks to make the crossroads look more like a tree house. It went on like that, trial after trial.

The proposition is that the normal human is compelled to interpret real behaviors and to construct a theory as to why they have occurred. Interpreting our behaviors would be a trivial matter if all behaviors we engaged in were the product of verbal conscious action. In that case, the source of the behavior is known before the action occurs. If all our actions consisted of only these kinds of events, there would be nothing to explain. I argue that the normal person does not possess a unitary conscious mechanism in which the conscious system is privy to the sources of all his or her actions. I want to build the argument that the normal brain is organized into modules and that most of these modules are capable of actions, moods, and responses. All except one work in nonverbal ways such that their modes of expression are solely through overt behaviors or more covert actions. To build this case I need more data, so let me continue.

In the laboratory we set the stage for other experiments on how the left brain interprets the responses of the right brain. This time we do not ask the right brain to make a real response, that is, carry out a real bodily movement. Instead, the right brain is given a list of words that it knows and that we know to be in the life of the patient. In the first part of the study, the right hemisphere is asked to judge on a seven-point scale of likability the value of each word. In this pretest the right brain responds by pointing to one of a set of seven cards that list the seven choices. It became quickly evident that the right brain liked some of the words and disliked others.

In the next phase of the experiment, again carried out by LeDoux and me, the manual response is not allowed.[5] Instead, the left has to speak out after each word is flashed to the right brain and give its one-to-seven rating of the word. In this situation, the left brain does not actually know what the word was that was presented. When it makes its guess it is responding to some feeling that is generated by the right brain and possibly communicated to the left through remaining brain pathways. The left brain's assessment of the words presented to the right

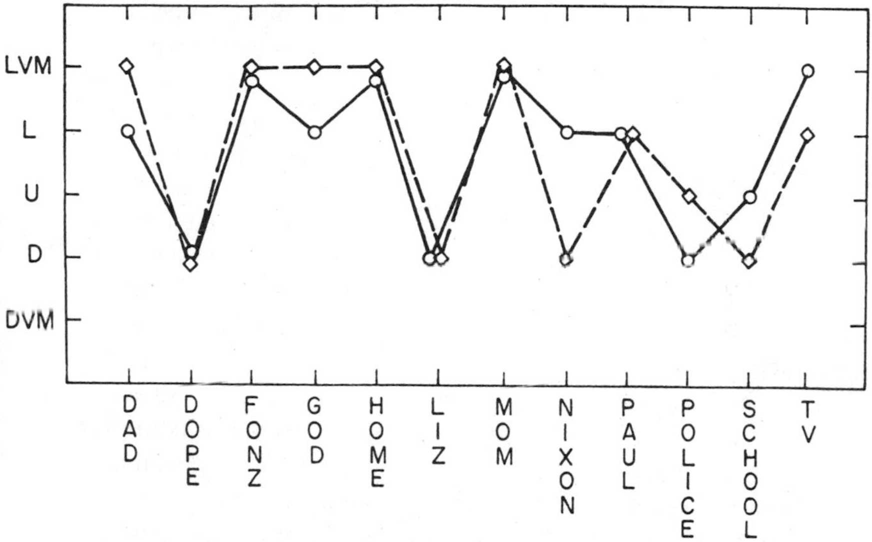

Figure 5.3. Left hemisphere verbal rating of stimuli exposed to the left and right hemispheres. Data points represented by open squares connected by dotted lines indicate right hemisphere exposure, and open circles connected by solid lines indicate left hemisphere exposure. In only one instance ("Nixon") did the ratings differ by more than one scale value.

LVM: like very much
L: like
U: undecided
D: dislike
DVM: dislike very much

SOURCE: Reprinted with permission from Michael S. Gazzaniga and Joseph LeDoux, *The Integrated Mind* (New York; Plenum, 1978).

was almost identical to those given by the right brain directly.

These experiments demonstrate that a separate mental system, in this case the right hemisphere, can react emotionally to a stimulus. It can put a valence, or value, on a stimulus and this value, either positive or negative, can be communicated to the left hemisphere's verbal system, yet the left hemisphere cannot say what the stimulus was that triggered the particular emotional response being analyzed (figure 5.3).

When Jeff Holtzman came to the lab he brought with him an

elaborate eye-tracking device designed by Tom Cornsweet at the Stanford Research Institute. It is a hugely complicated machine that requires a computer and hundreds of thousands of dollars worth of software to run. His mentor, Leon Festinger, had changed fields of interest and had no need for it, so he sent it along with Holtzman. The machine would have been useless without Holtzman and six computer jockeys he knew in New York who also know how to run it. In their hands it works perfectly and allows us to conduct many new experiments, not only on the split-brain patients but also on other neurological cases.

The machine precisely measures the movement of the eyes. If the subject, while sitting in the tracker, moves his or her eyes even an iota, the computer closes an electronic shutter. This in turn stops a movie being shown to either the right or the left brain. In other words, the machine allows us to present a sustained visual story to one hemisphere or the other. It gives us time to create a mood.

In tests on V.P., who has the best-shaped eyeball for the machine to read, we were able to show her, for one or two minutes at a time, film clips that produced emotional reactions.[6] In the first tests we showed her a filmstrip from the Cornell Office of Health and Safety, which counsels its employees not to throw fellow employees into fires should they come across one. This bit of drama brought to us by some federal regulation is indeed terrifying. V.P. saw it, thanks to the eye tracker, only with her then mute right hemisphere. This was the exchange that occurred between her and me, the examiner.

M.S.G.: What did you see?

V.P.: I don't really know what I saw. I think just a white flash.

M.S.G.: Were there people in it?

V.P.: I don't think so. Maybe just some trees, red trees like in the fall.

M.S.G.: Did it make you feel any emotion?

V.P.: I don't really know why but I'm kind of scared. I feel jumpy. I think maybe I don't like this room, or maybe it's you. You're getting me nervous.

V.P. then turned to an assistant and said, "I know I like Dr. Gazzaniga, but right now I'm scared of him for some reason."

When a more serene view was presented such as a filmstrip of the ocean in front of my house in Santa Barbara, V.P. talked on about how she thought the picture was "nice and calm." Here again the left half-brain was correctly reading the overall mood generated by the mute right half-brain. It is important to note that either end of the affective scale could be so appreciated. From distress to serenity the left half-brain appreciated the emotional state of the right half-brain. The phenomenon is as dramatic as it sounds. Let me review the position.

The split-brain patient allows us to conduct discrete experiments that examine how two separate mental systems interact. This is a convenience for research and must not be mistaken as the way the normal brain works. The two halves of the brain are normally linked together, and the phenomena I have described accounts for a special instance. Yet I am arguing that this special instance gives a much more general insight into normal brain organization. My interpretation is that the normal brain is organized into modular-processing systems, hundreds of them or maybe even thousands, and that these modules can usually express themselves only through real action, not through verbal communication. Most of these systems, not unlike those existing in animals, can remember events, store affective reactions to those events, and respond to stimuli associated with a particular memory. All of these activities are routinely carried out by cats, dogs, and apes, and by humans. These activities proceed without language and with abandon. They are the elements that a functioning mental system draws upon for a complete mental life. Consider an example of everyday life that fits into my argument.

It is a Monday evening at home. All seems in place, all is well. You are chatting with friends, everybody is feeling cheerful, and everything is going your way. Then waking on Tuesday, your mood has darkened for no apparent reason, and you wonder what happened. The data about life's good fortunes have not been altered in the last twelve hours. Why the change?

I would argue that a nonverbal module has somehow been activated, and the emotional associates of the events stored in that module have been communicated to the brain's emotional system. What we all tend to forget is that the rich capacity of the vertebrate brain to learn conditioned associative responses is an active brain function that humans have in common with all the nonspeaking subhuman vertebrates such as your pet dog. Humans are constantly being conditioned to have particular emotional responses, and the particular modules in the brain that store that information can become activated for expression by any of a number of means.

In this particular case of the Tuesday morning blues, a negative mood is felt. If you let the process stop there, life might be a lot simpler. What I am arguing is that you begin to interpret previously neutral, negative, or even positive events more negatively as a result of having to explain this new mood. Alas, the person lying next to you might be in for a real surprise.

This example deals with the subtle manipulations of mood and how they interact to change one's beliefs about things, people, and events. My claim, however, extends to overt behaviors.[7] The phenomenon is ubiquitous. Consider the happily married man who believes in fidelity. The Christmas party comes along and after a little too much cheer he winds up in bed next to Suzy. He proceeds to participate in a behavior that is at odds with his beliefs about the social institution he has contracted to be a part of. What happens? How does he explain his behavior?

What happens, of course, is that he changes his evaluation of the importance of fidelity to marriage through a powerful psychological mechanism which has been brilliantly articulated

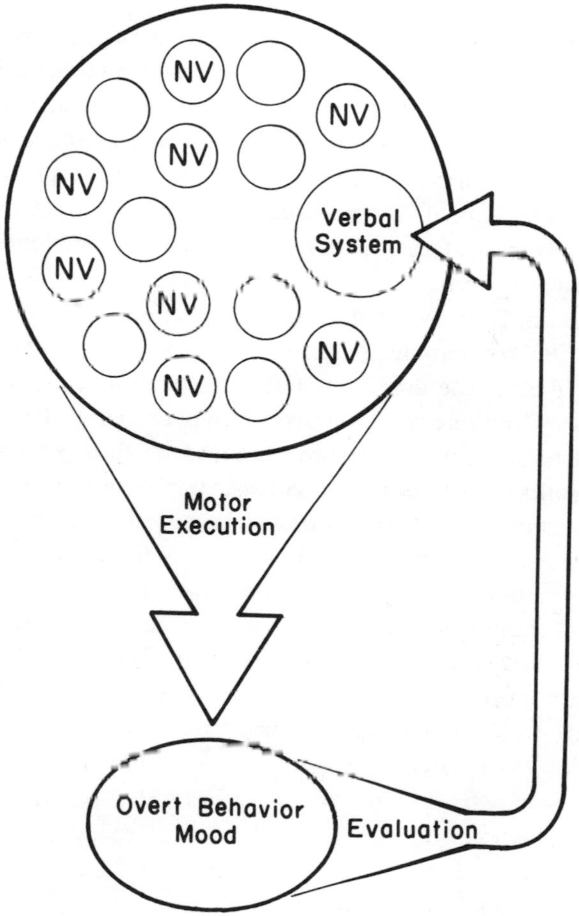

Figure 5.4. The many observations on split-brain patients all lead to the conclusion that the brain is organized in a modular fashion with each module capable of producing independent behaviors. Once the behaviors are emitted, the left-hemisphere language-based system interprets the behavior and constructs a theory as to its meaning.
(NV: Nonverbal)

by Leon Festinger.[8] Because people cannot live in a state of dissonance between a held belief and an actual behavior, something has to give, and it is usually the value of the belief. That is the gist of Festinger's theory of cognitive dissonance.

What the new brain science brings to this interpretation is the knowledge about how the brain is organized, that in fact it is organized in these relatively independent modules that are capable of initiating the disparate behavior in the first place. The implications of this model of mind will be dealt with shortly. For now let me simply summarize the discovery (see figure 5.4). The dominant left hemisphere is committed to the task of interpreting our overt behaviors as well as the more covert emotional responses produced by these separate mental modules of our brain. It constructs theories as to why these behaviors occurred and does so because of that brain system's need to maintain a sense of consistency for all of our behaviors. It is a uniquely human endeavor, and upon it rests not only the mechanism that generates our sense of subjective reality but also a mental capacity to free us from the binding controls of external contingencies. I believe this point to be of fundamental importance and will describe supporting data in the next chapter.

CHAPTER 6

The Search for Modularity

TWO THOUSAND YEARS of Western thought has urged the view that our actions are the product of a unitary conscious system. This represents a rather substantive body of opinion, and there are many institutions and scientific beliefs built up around this assumption. To effectively challenge this view takes time, great effort, and always more supporting data. Let me return to the neurologic clinic, this time to other kinds of patients, problems, and test procedures. My objective is to bring to your attention other converging experimental data that argue for the modular view of mind.

There is a procedure in neuroradiology called angiography. In this procedure an opaque dye is injected into the brain vessels and X rays are taken. The result is a picture of the normal or abnormal blood supply to the brain. It is an extremely useful procedure and particularly helpful to the neurosurgeon.

In a similar procedure called the Wada test, invented many years ago by Canadian neurosurgeon Juin Wada, a short-acting anesthetic is injected into the brain arteries.[1] Because of the way the brain vessels are organized, the drug is delivered to one hemisphere and not to the other. (This brief general description will suffice for our present purpose, although there are a host of qualifications for it.) The technique allows one hemisphere to be put to sleep temporarily while the other remains awake. It was devised in order to assure the neurosurgeon that the hemisphere that should be dominant for language is, in fact, dominant. The test should cause the left hemisphere, usually dominant for language, to be unable to respond to spoken commands or to produce speech. When the drug is injected into the nondominant hemisphere, these processes are not interfered with. Sometimes there are surprises, and it is important to be absolutely sure which hemisphere is dominant for language if major neurosurgery is contemplated.

It would be unfair to the reader not to communicate the excitement of many of the research procedures that produce the kinds of observations being offered here. One of the most compelling scenes I have experienced occurs in the medical suite of the neuroradiologist during the Wada test. It is worth describing.

The patient, who is normal except for some type of acquired brain damage—brain tumor, aneurysm (a thin arterial wall in danger of bursting), or an a-v malformation (a strange pathological network of vessels at the junction where oxygenated arterial blood blends into deoxygenated venous blood)—is laid fully conscious on a mechanical table. The table is electronically controlled so that the patient can be moved horizontally under an X-ray machine, allowing pictures to be taken of his body and head. The attending doctors all wear lead aprons in the examination room to avoid excessive exposure to radiation, especially to their testes.

Originally, a needle was placed directly into the carotid artery, which runs along the side of the neck. The left carotid represents the main feed to the left hemisphere and the right carotid is the main feed to the right hemisphere. This method was stopped when, in a few cases, the needle removed a substance (called a plaque) from the arterial wall which was subsequently pumped into the brain, causing a blockage or infarct and resulting in a stroke. Now a catheter is put into an artery in the leg and fed up through the chest into the neck and finally into the carotid artery on one side of the brain. This way, if the introduction of the needle into artery causes a plaque to loosen, an artery in the leg is blocked, something far more tolerable than a blockage in an artery of the brain.

The neuroradiologist inserts the catheter and tracks its way up to the brain, guiding it through the arteries and steering it clear of detours and culs-de-sac. The patient watches the catheter's progress on the same TV monitor the doctor uses. It is an electrifying event.

Finally when the catheter is in place, the Wada test is ready to begin. The patient's hands are held straight up in the air. When the drug takes effect, the hand opposite the anesthetized hemisphere falls down in a state of transient paralysis. The other hemisphere is awake, as is the motor apparatus of the opposite side of the body. The stage is set for the psychologist to once again piggy-back on a medical procedure and ask a question about brain organization.

Take the case of a patient who is not aphasic but who is having his left hemisphere put to sleep for two or three minutes. The neuroradiologist injects the drug into the left carotid artery and after about twenty-five seconds the left brain no longer understands language and the right hand is paralyzed. The room becomes very tense because this procedure is a manipulation of human consciousness. The left hand is mobile and sentient because the right brain is awake. I place an object (a spoon) in the speechless person's sentient hand, ask him to remember it, and remove it after about thirty seconds.

A few minutes pass, the drug begins to wear off, and the patient gradually regains consciousness. I ask, "How do you feel?" The patient's usual response is "very good," as the drug gives a "high" along with its other effects. I then say, "I placed something in your left hand while you were asleep. Can you tell me what it was?" The patient looks puzzled and usually denies anything had been presented to his left hand. This is the left brain's language system trying to access information that exists in the brain but is tucked away in some kind of code or mental module that does not recognize the brain processes that represent natural language. I pursue, "Are you sure you don't remember anything I gave you a few minutes ago?" Again a denial of knowledge.

I then show the patient a group of objects, one of which I had put in the left hand minutes before. With decisive speed the patient points to the correct object and then adds, "Oh yes, it was the spoon," in much the same fashion as one of our split-brain patients theorizes with the left hemisphere about movements initiated by the right.

What does all this mean? In a way, what we have done is slip some information into the brain without the language system's awareness.[2] The information becomes encoded in the brain in one of the many mental modules that records experiences. It is not, however, one that talks. In fact, when language processes return, the module does not tell its secrets to the language system. Whether or not this is because the information is in a neural code without access to another, much as an Italian has a hard time understanding a Greek, I do not know. Whatever the final mechanism proves to be, this kind of experience does show how information can exist in the brain, can be ready and able to express itself through movement, and at the same time be unavailable to the language system. The results add weight to the theory of multiple mental modules.

Let me present another line of evidence.[3] A bizarre clinical finding is that patients with a lesion in the posterior regions of the right hemisphere do not see information presented in their left visual field if other information is simultaneously presented in their right visual field. For example, imagine yourself looking straight on at such a patient, head to head. If you held up a comb in your left hand and an apple in your right hand, the patient would maintain that he or she saw only the comb. Patients "extinguish" the apple (see figure 6.1).

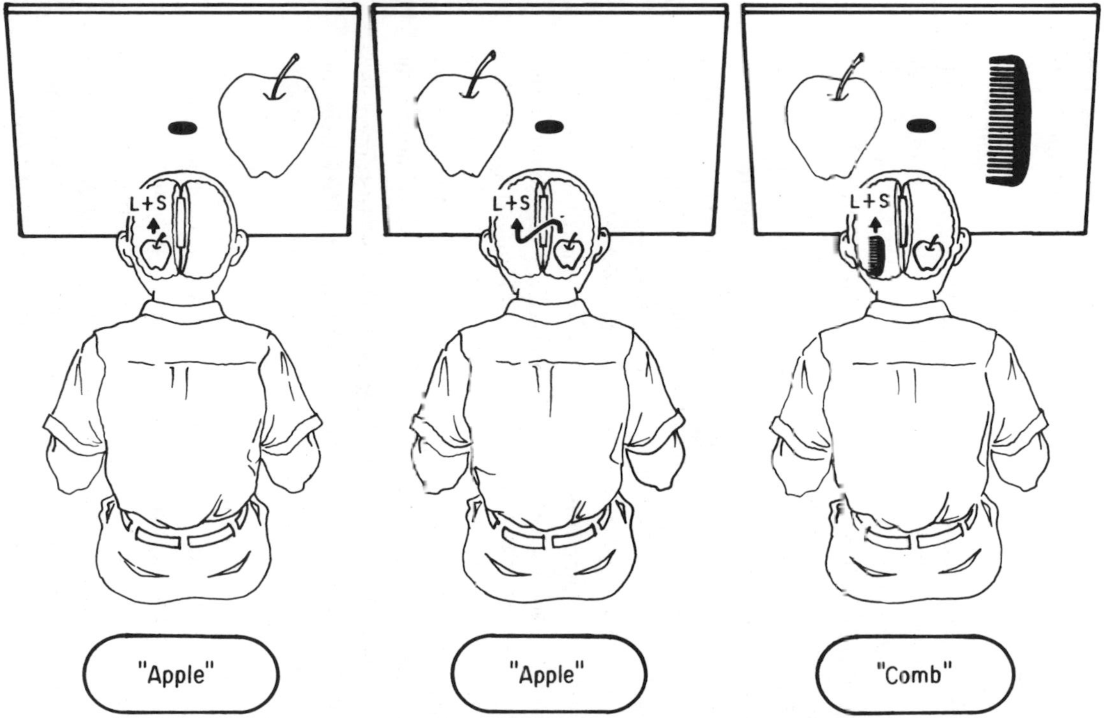

Figure 6.1. It is a common occurrence when examining patients with right-hemisphere lesions to observe what is called "extinction." When information is presented to either side of the visual midline alone, they name it just like a normal control subject does. Yet when two objects are placed in front of them, they "extinguish" the picture in the left visual field and claim only to see the information in the right visual field. (L and S stand for language and speech in the left hemisphere.)

The first question asked in such a situation is whether or not the patient is actually blind. Does the brain lesion affect the visual system such that the information is not reaching the brain in the first place? The answer is no, because if a single object (stimulus) is held up in the extinguished field, the patient is perfectly able to report on it. So the question becomes, what happens to that visual information under the condition of behavioral stimulation that the patient cannot verbally describe? Can the information be used in a computation even though the verbal system does not have access to it?

The answer is that it most certainly can. If we ask the patient not to name what the two stimuli are, but merely to state whether the two objects are the same or different, the patient is able to make that judgment. Remarkably, on the trials where the stimuli are different and they say so, they cannot name the stimulus that is presented in the extinguished visual field. In other words, a computation transpires in one of the mental modules, and the product of the computation is delivered to the verbal system. The verbal system can take advantage of the answer but cannot tell you what went into the calculation. It is a compelling observation.

Once again the data suggest that the brain is organized in such a way that information is stored in modules. These modules can compute, remember, feel emotion, and act. They exist in such a way that they need not be in touch with the natural language and cognitive systems underlying private conscious experience. In a broader sense, what we hold as conscious experiences are, to a large extent, the verbally tagged memories that are associated with the interpretations we have given to our behaviors.

The neurologic clinic is full of rich examples that point to the modular view. Last year we saw a patient whom I'll call Mrs. Smith, who had a lesion in her right parietal zone. Lesions in this location can produce a wide variety of disturbances, among them Mrs. Smith's translocation of place. She was a patient of

Dr. Jerome Posner of Memorial Sloan-Kettering in New York City.[4] He called one day to say that we had to see this patient and, because of her symptoms, we videotaped the testing session.

Mrs. Smith was in Memorial Hospital for brain surgery. Although she was an intelligent woman with great charm and wit, she believed herself to be in Freeport, Maine. She sat in hospital garb in her wheelchair with an IV in place, and during the course of a conversation about the intricacies of American history she would respond to the question, "By the way, Mrs. Smith, where are you?" by saying, "I am in Freeport, Maine. Where are you?" When I pointed to the elevators and asked, "What are those things over there?" she would respond, "Those are elevators. Do you know what it cost me to have those put in my house? You know ever since I came in to have my brain surgery, every doctor that has walked into my room has asked me where I am, and every time I tell them I am in Freeport, Maine. Every time they correct me and tell me I am at Memorial Sloan-Kettering in New York. Finally, after about a week of this, Dr. Posner said to me just say you are in New York. They didn't care whether or not I believe it."

Here is an otherwise intelligent woman with a module malfunctioning as the result of her brain disease. That module contributed some unique data concerning her real-time location in space. Its malfunction forced her into the position of having to explain some bizarre realities in reference to her location in space, and she did this with little hesitation.

Until 1978, my general formulation about the existence of mental modules evolved from considering the results of experiments on split-brain patients and other clinical populations such as Mrs. Smith. However, in that year a most extraordinary development occurred. It came about first in one of the split-brain patients, Case P.S. His right hemisphere began to talk, and with that a whole new era of observations began.

Ordinarily a split-brain patient is able to name information presented in the right visual field, but not in the left. Imagine my surprise and delight when P.S. began to name information presented into the left visual field. He was our breakthrough case, and he had had his surgery only three years before.[5]

The first question to be asked about this is whether this really is right-brain speech or whether the information being presented to the right brain is somehow being transferred over to the left, talking hemisphere? Consider the situation. A picture of a fork is shown to the left hemisphere and a key is shown to the right. P.S. immediately says, "fork and key" (see figure 6.2). But if you ask the usual split-brain patient, "Are the two pictures I am about to show you the same or different?" he or she is unable to do the task above a chance level. This is because mind left sees a fork and mind right sees a key and for all practical purposes they do not communicate with each other. It is just as if I showed a key to person A and a fork to person B. Unless they talked to each other, there is no way one of them could guess above a chance level whether or not they were both presented the same object.

When a patient speaks from both hemispheres, our picture of who is explaining what to whom becomes more complicated. Fortunately it remains the case that the left hemisphere is still the dominant partner in this relationship; it does most of the talking. The right brain is prone to one-line descriptions, as can be seen from the results of another experiment. This study also brings us right back to the persistent characteristic of the left brain, that it constructs a theory about behaviors emitted, and in this case the behavior is language coming from the right half-brain.

In this study, P.S. was shown a series of slides with two words on each slide (see figure 6.3).[6] When read normally from left to right the series of slides told a logical story (Story 1. Mary + Ann, May + Come, Visit + Into, The + Town, Ship + Today). P.S., of course, could not read the story from left to right; instead, on a given trial each hemisphere received a single word. The left hemisphere proceeded to read only the words on the

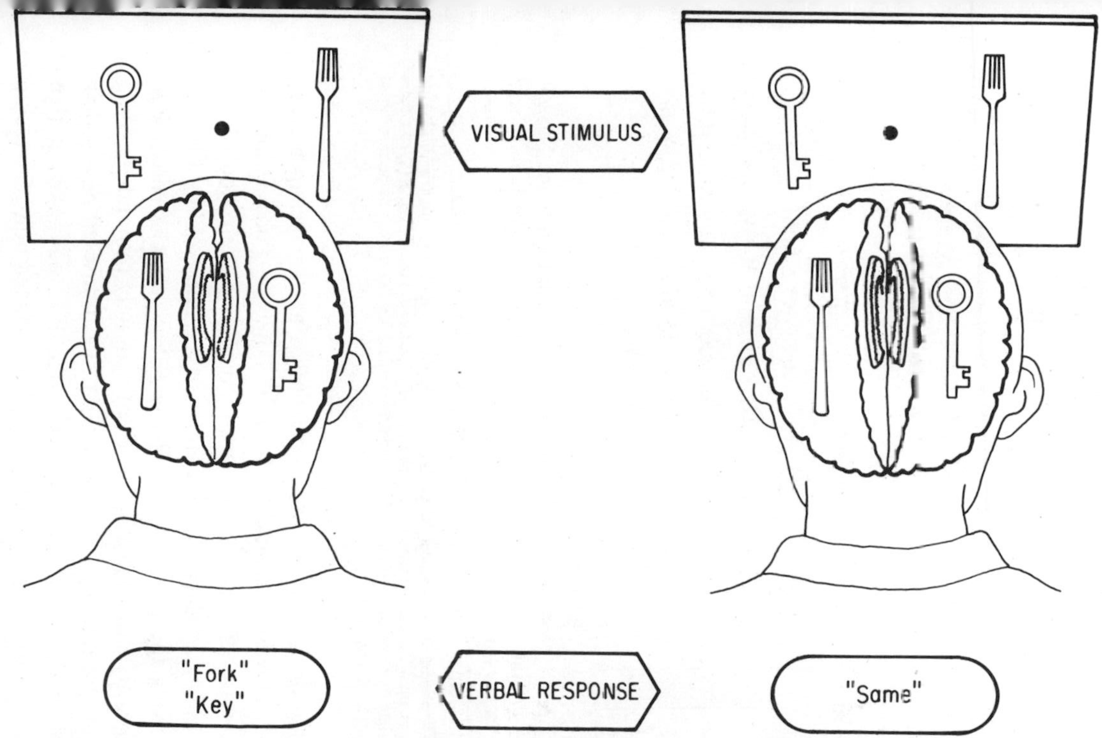

Figure 6.2. In patients with the capacity to speak out of each half-brain, such as patients P.S. and V.P., stimulus arrays as seen here are quickly named because each hemisphere can describe the picture presented to it. Yet if the patients are asked not to name the objects but rather to judge whether the two objects presented are the same or different, they are unable to do so because neither hemisphere knows what the other hemisphere saw unless it is named out loud.

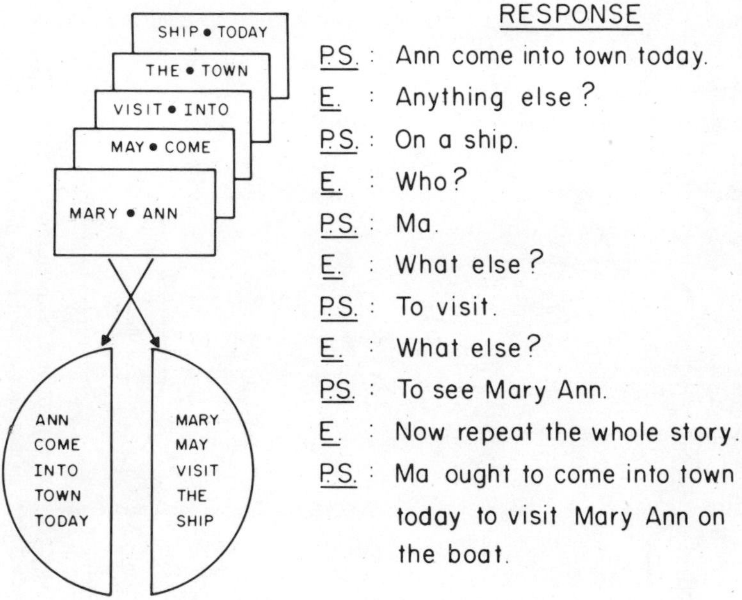
SHIP • TODAY
THE • TOWN
VISIT • INTO
MAY • COME
MARY • ANN
ANN
COME
INTO
TOWN
TODAY
MARY
MAY
VISIT
THE
SHIP
RESPONSE
P.S. : Ann come into town today.
E. : Anything else?
P.S. : On a ship.
E. : Who?
P.S. : Ma.
E. : What else?
P.S. : To visit.
E. : What else?
P.S. : To see Mary Ann.
E. : Now repeat the whole story.
P.S. : Ma ought to come into town today to visit Mary Ann on the boat.

Figure 6.3. Two stories are presented, one to each half-brain. The left hemisphere quickly reports its story, followed by the right hemisphere offering its story in bits and pieces. After the left brain hears these semantic items, it combines both stories into yet a new one.

SOURCE: Reprinted from Michael S. Gazzaniga, "Right Hemisphere Language Following Brain Bisection: A 20-Year Perspective," *American Psychologist*, vol. 38, no. 5 (1983): 525–37. Copyright 1983 by the American Psychological Association. Reprinted by permission of the author and publisher.

right side of the screen, which by design also make up a story (Story 2. + Ann, + Come, + Into, + Town, + Today), and the right hemisphere read only the words on the left side of the screen (Story 3. Mary +, May +, Visit +, The +, Ship +).

Following the presentation of the entire series of slides, P.S. was asked to recall the story. He immediately responded, "Ann come into town today." This was the more robust left hemisphere expressing what it had perceived. Then P.S. was asked if that was the full story. He paused briefly and blurted out, "On a ship . . . to visit . . . to visit Ma." When asked to repeat the whole story, he replied, "Ann came into town today to visit Ma on the boat."

Once again we see the integration of disparate behaviors into a coherent framework. With the development of bilateral access to speech, behaviors generated by the right hemisphere, which now initiate the spoken word, are incorporated into the conscious stream of the left hemisphere.

A still simpler test was carried out on V.P. after she began to speak from the right hemisphere.[7] Line drawings of scenes were presented either to her left or to her right hemisphere. The drawings were more complicated than just a picture of an apple. Instead, they were, for example, a hurdler jumping over a hurdle with a particular set of clothes on and headed in a specific direction. When one of these pictures was presented to the left brain, it was described in accurate detail. When presented to the right, the form of the description was different. Whereas the initial characterization was accurate, for example, "athlete," the follow-up description went further and further afield. Instead of being a hurdler, the description might have been of a basketball player. In this situation we meet our old friend again. The left half-brain hears the word "athlete" come out of its own mouth and invents a stimulus to explain its response. The phenomenon is extraordinary, and we see it all the time.

Results of testing under conditions of strict behavior manipulation lead to intriguing suppositions regarding the normal subject. To take a simpler example first, we can all remember blurting out some word or statement, usually as the result of some kind of imagined loss of self-control, and then attempting to overcome the embarrassment it caused. This usually results in worsening the situation by elaborating on the remark. I am thinking of the times when we surprise ourselves at how angry we become at something that is said in our presence. Controlling the unleashed emotion frequently becomes a severe challenge.

The more interesting case is one that is rankly speculative but is more closely related to the subtle and usually opaque process of creative cognition. It has to do with the process of writing. I believe it is usually the case that a writer is not fully aware of what the import of a sentence, paragraph, or page will be. The writing process, which elicits mental images through the judicious use of words, demonstrates how different thoughts are from their written form. Where do we find the words to capture and convey the peculiar quality of our personal communications? Why does the written version of our ideas appear different from what we first imagined we wished to say?

A few years ago George Miller and I were having an evening drink at the Rockefeller University Faculty Club when we decided it would be a good idea to discuss this paradox with professional *users* of language instead of with professional scientists, who merely *think* about language. (Miller has not only thought about language in a profound sense, he is able to write fine prose.)

We invited a group of distinguished authors—William Buckley, Tom Wicker, and Tom Wolfe—to a dinner party for a discussion of this linguistic phenomenon. We had also invited John Updike, who typed a note saying that unfortunately he would not be able "to be at our table." He had first written "to be at our dinner" and then crossed out "dinner" for the preferred word. I liked that because it confirmed my idea that great writing is a product of great editing—a view I expressed at our "table." That view, however, did not convince the others present. Tom Wolfe declared that (a) it took twenty years to learn how to write and (b) he himself precasts each page in his mind's eye and rarely does any editing. It was a grand dinner. Miller guided these cultural giants through the problems of teaching language skills to our best college students. He was very good at explaining things since he can identify and verbalize a problem with incredible skill, and he does not express his opinions until he has developed his ideas to his own satisfaction.

Let me propose a model of the cognitive processes that accompany writing. As sentences are formed, the words begin to elicit mental images, each accessing related images carrying different emotional valences. This fluctuating state of emotional energy leads to description of all these images by the continually active verbal system. In this dynamic way, the initial action is modified.

It is an idea worth considering because, as I am about to show, language is a system that is not intrinsically powerful. Language reports the cognitive computations of other mental modules. If I can convincingly establish this link, then the foregoing has more than a little substance.

A major challenge to the student of human cognition is to determine what language qua language confers on overall cognitive processes. At an elementary level, it is eminently reasonable that specific knowledge of a word and its meaning aids personal comprehension enormously. Consider the word "vainglorious." To someone hearing the word and unsure of its meaning, it might sound like a cumbersome phonetic ensemble that need not exist in our language. We all know what "vain" means and we all know what "glorious" means and we all can imagine what the hybrid might mean. Yet when we hear the definition, "excessive or ostentatious pride, especially in one's achievements," the word takes on an exacting reflection of a thought. It is so exacting that the obvious conclusion is that something about words and their definitions actually facilitates cognition. I am going to argue that this is not correct.

Psychologists have traditionally tried to discern the relation between language and cognition by studying, during different stages in their development, children in whom the two processes are in various decoupled states.[8] The literature on this subject is perplexing because a cognitive system and a language system may be co-evolving, making it very difficult to interpret conclusions about dissociations that one comes across.

Another method commonly employed to investigate the link between language and cognitive processes is to study the language and cognition capability of the chimpanzee.[9] David Premack has carried out ingenious studies on this animal. The rationale for his approach is straightforward and seemingly plausible: in order to learn what is unique about the human species, determine the capabilities of its closest ancestor. Try to figure out how language training might help it to solve otherwise unsolvable problems. When the study is complete, those features of mental life that can be carried out only by our species will be so identified.

The problem I have always had with this approach is that what appear to be similar acts of man and beast may not, in fact, be the same. When my pet dog runs out the door at 6:00 A.M. to visit the deli on First Avenue for a dish of milk, and when I go out much later for my quart of milk, a Martian might think we are engaged in the same act for the same reason, supported by the same brain systems in each of us. Nothing could be further from the truth.

The problem of establishing a common vocabulary applicable to man studying humans is extremely difficult. It is the same as in a political discussion with a Soviet, since his use of the words "freedom," "democracy," and the like mean totally different things from what Westerners mean by these concepts.

Once we identify our target for study—the biological and psychological nature of our own species, *Homo sapiens sapiens*—then *Homo sapiens sapiens* is the species we should study. The biosphere leading up to modern *Homo sapiens sapiens* man is of enormous interest and studies on every conceivable aspect and on every possible topic, from cellular genetics to the capacity of animals to form affective bonds, has contributed to setting the context for understanding ourselves. But, again, to understand humans you must study humans.

Another approach is the one used by the cognitive neuroscientist, whose subject is usually the aphasic patient. As already mentioned, this patient usually has suffered a stroke in the left half-brain that caused language impairment. When language understanding is impaired, so too is cognition. The greater the disturbance to language comprehension, the greater the cognitive impairment. These data are typically interpreted as showing that language and cognition are hopelessly linked phenomena.

I wanted to test this idea on our three special split-brain patients. Remember, the right brain of man does not normally possess language. Our three patients, for reasons that are unclear, do possess right-hemisphere language, and since the two hemispheres are disconnected, we can study what language confers to a neural system that does not normally possess it. Does language let the right hemisphere do all the things it lets the left hemisphere do? Well, that is not quite the way to put it. One might want to ask whether in a right brain with language, language almost as measurably rich as that of the left brain, cognition exists at the same level. It does not.

Let me quickly review how facile the language system is in these three patients. All three possess rich lexicons, the right not being significantly different from the left. Two patients can also carry out some syntactic processing and two can speak as well as understand language with the right hemisphere.

This quick summary does not communicate the spellbinding dimensions of these very special people. Let me give a fascinating example from J.W.'s history. J.W. is a patient who understands both written and spoken language in the right brain, but cannot as yet speak from it. I flash a word to his right brain and in order for him to indicate that he grasped the word and its various meanings, I simply ask him to "Draw with your left hand a picture of the word I flashed." In the beginning of any one test session he usually protests that my command doesn't make any sense because he (the left brain) has not seen anything (which it hasn't) so how can he draw something. I nurse him along and say something like, "Oh, Joe, go ahead and let that left hand try." The left hand will pick up a pencil and accurately draw a picture representing the word flashed (see figure 6.4). He does this kind of thing routinely.

It is of interest to note that when a word or a picture has been

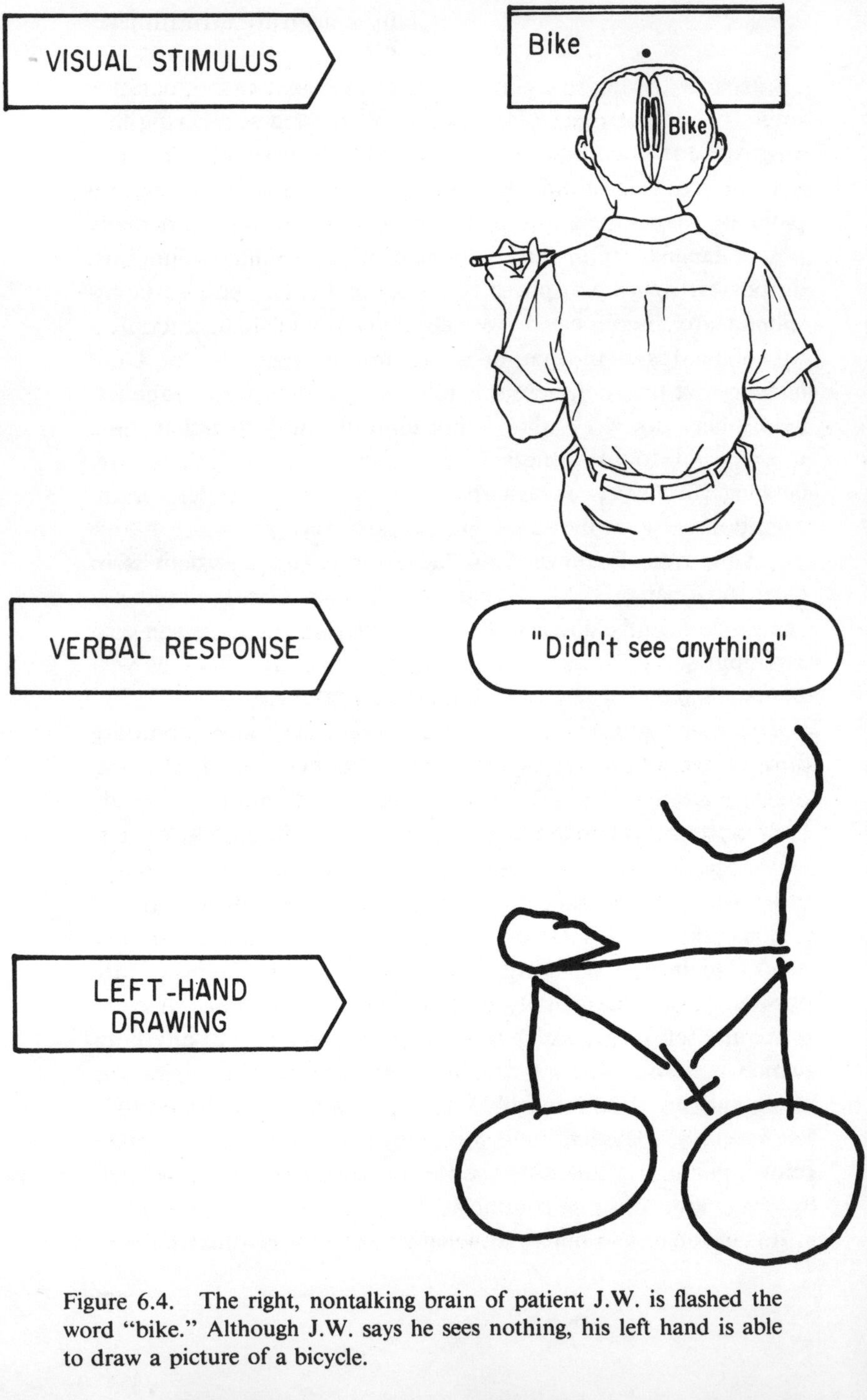

Figure 6.4. The right, nontalking brain of patient J.W. is flashed the word "bike." Although J.W. says he sees nothing, his left hand is able to draw a picture of a bicycle.

presented to only the right brain and the left hand draws the answer, J.W. will typically say, "I don't know why I drew that. What is it? It looks like a bird. I guess I saw a bird." This is a test situation where the left brain saw nothing. It has received no stimulus and the interpretation of the action is more circuitous and less dramatic than in the double-field presentation situations described at the beginning of the chapter. Yet it is still there.

To further demonstrate the language power of this right brain, suppose that instead of having J.W. draw a picture of the word he saw I say, "Joe, don't draw a picture of the word. Draw me a picture of what goes on it." If I flash the word "horse," J.W. picks up the pencil and draws not the horse, but a beautiful but abstract picture of a saddle. I then say, "Draw a picture of what the word was," and out comes a picture of a horse. At that, Joe says, "Oh, I guess this thing is a saddle." (See figure 6.5.)

We know from other tests that J.W.'s right brain does not understand syntactic niceties. But it has enough pragmatic language knowledge to listen and follow my instructions. If one simply observed how J.W.'s right brain responded to my questions, one would say it qualifies as being conscious in the human sense of that word. Nevertheless, this half-brain with all of these language qualities cannot make a simple inference.

If I flash the words "pin" and "finger" to the right brain, and J.W.'s task is to combine the words into a new meaning or to make a simple inference about those two words, the right brain fails miserably. The task is simple because the answer, in this case the word "bleed," is listed in front of the patient along with other possible choices. J.W. responds at random from the right brain; the left brain, of course, finds the task trivial. What is even more astounding is that the right brain, if flashed the word "bleed," can define it. Other inabilities are as great. The right brain cannot carry out simple math. It cannot solve second-grade geometric puzzles. What can we conclude? We can start by observing that a rich language system does not necessarily mean rich cognition exists. Language qua language confers little.

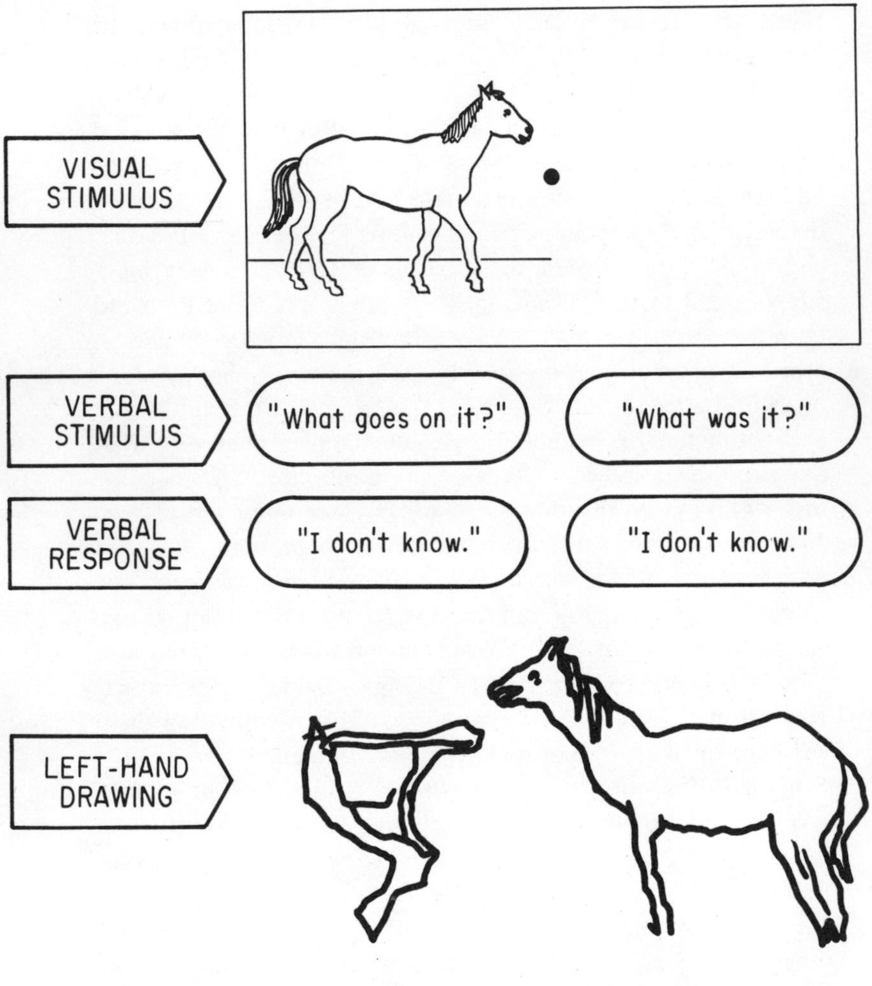

Figure 6.5. In this example of right-hemisphere comprehension, J.W. was asked not to draw what he actually saw, but instead to draw a picture of "what goes on it." J.W. drew an English saddle. Subsequently he was asked to draw what he saw.

There are other systems coincident with language that do the serious computing and decision making. Language merely reports on these other processes. These processes exist alongside language in the left hemisphere but seem absent in the right brain.

There are unique neural systems present in the left hemisphere of (right-handed) humans that compel the brain system communicating with the external world to make sense out of the diverse behaviors humans produce. Inherent in this process is the person's developing "beliefs" about the nature of the self, which become more multidimensional the more diverse the mental modules are in their behaviors. These beliefs take on a central importance to the person and as such can override the tugs on the person produced by more mundanely delivered rewards or punishments for the behavior.

I argue further that the presence of beliefs in our species results from the way the human brain is constructed. With the appearance of left-hemisphere systems that allow for the making of inference, an act that freed humans from the endless tedium of advancing by trial and error, the system was inextricably committed to the construction of human beliefs. A brain system that can make inference about events in the real world must by definition make inferences about its own behaviors. Once beliefs were in place, the organism no longer lived only in the present. The montage of conditioned responses that had governed biological creatures for all of time now dwelt in a brain system capable of thwarting their power.

CHAPTER 7

Modularity and Memory

A SINGULARLY important task in the scientific process is to check and recheck all of one's own experiments and to constantly look for other experimental settings to try to confirm or disconfirm hypotheses. Proposing that the brain is organized in modular form makes certain predictions that can be examined in a variety of patient groups. The main prediction is that strange and striking dissociations in various behaviors should be observable. Nowhere is the phenomenon more evident than in the study of amnesia.

Amnesia is not only the stuff of popular suspense novels. It is a clinical state that has been carefully studied for decades by a host of talented neuropsychologists. How the brain stores information and through what kind of logical structure it retrieves information is about as exciting an intellectual question as one can address. How is it, for example, that the brain (you) can almost instantly recognize that "secleb" is not a word in the English language. Depending on your level of knowledge of English you might have as many as two hundred and fifty thousand words in your working vocabulary. "Secleb" could be a word. It has all of the proper phonemic and graphemic elements of a word, yet, you instantly knew that it was not. Why didn't your brain have to look in its dictionary word by word before it rendered a decision? Why is it the more a human (brain) knows the faster it works, while the more an artifact (computer) knows the slower it works?

Colleagues in experimental psychology working with intact normal brains have been examining these exciting and other related questions for years. Before I get to the neuropsychological work done with amnesiacs, it is worth pointing out that much of our understanding of memory processes came from experimental psychologists studying normal brains. Indeed, they have carefully charted the processes of memory and have made a number of crucial observations. There are, for example, processes that seem to work very quickly on new information. These processes control (and limit) the amount of information one can apprehend with only a brief exposure to stimuli. Still other short-term processes allow one to rehearse new information, such as someone's telephone number, and with a little practice commit it to long-term memory. Other processes work on how a memory is retrieved from long-term storage. The experimental psychologists, usually working with normal college sophomores as their subject base, always push the normal brain until the system breaks down so that errors are made by the subject. Also, the length of time a subject takes to perform certain tasks is carefully measured, and through such strategies the resulting patterns of errors and latency differences allow the psychologist to construct theories about how the memory system must work.

I first became interested in how the brain represented human memories some years ago after my father had suffered a small but transiently disabling stroke in his left hemisphere. Within twenty-four hours he changed from a vibrant, energetic man to one near death. He became totally aphasic, unable to carry out even the simplest written or spoken command. This event was most distressing, as disabling diseases are the hardest to bear. All of his children went home to him, and the family stood on twenty-four-hour watch in his room.

Then, suddenly, the entire disabling process started to reverse itself. My father began to move, to show signs of becoming sentient. Over the course of a few days, all of his faculties returned, including his delicious sense of humor. It turned out the stroke was an infarct of a small arterial branch of one of the brain's posterior arteries, and the net effect had been to cause more swelling to surrounding tissue than any actual damage. As the swelling subsided, the surrounding neural tissue and networks began to function once again.

It was during this time of recovery that I was able to make a set of observations that caused me to think about what I used to call the multidimensionality of human memories. The actual observations were as follows. At one point in time as he was recovering, I asked Dad to name for me a set of items in the room. Everything was going fine until I held up a carnation. He said he didn't know what it was. He told me it was a flower, that it was pink, and then he took it from me with a big smile and placed it in his lapel. Still, he couldn't name it. I then said three words, one of which was "carnation," and asked him to indicate which item it was. He was unable to do so. I then told him it was a carnation and he said, "Okay, if you say so."

Moments later I asked him if he remembered what plant we had planted at his Santa Barbara house the preceding weekend. He said, "Oh yes, it was Sunday afternoon, Becky was there, and we planted it down by the Lewis house near the southeast corner of the property." I said, "Yeah, but what was the name of the plant?" He couldn't guess even though he was a fabulous gardener and it was a gazania, a plant he loved both aesthetically and phonetically. Naming it for him didn't help either. About six hours later all of this cleared. He proceeded to name every plant in the room and its genus and species.

Clearly his mending brain was at a particular stage during the time of the examination, which resulted in what psychologists call a nice "dissociation." At the time when he couldn't name the flower he could give all other relevant information about the item. The circuits, modules that process these aspects of the stimulus, were functioning. The module or neural circuit that stored the actual name was nonfunctioning. It wasn't simply a naming problem because, although he could name other items with ease, he did not recognize a particular item even when it was named for him. These kinds of observations not only argue for modularity, they suggest that the modularities are highly specific. Time, space, affect, and a host of other dimensions of a stimulus event all have to be encoded, and apparently are encoded, in different brain areas.[1]

Still, such observations are informal and must be followed up with direct experimentation. The bedside exam can give clues, but the real data are from formal experiments. Years after my father's stroke, my lab became involved in real studies on amnesia in the context of existing research in amnesia, about which there is much to say.

Around 1950 modern clinical work started on this topic with the strange history of Case H.M.[2] He was a patient of the Hartford neurosurgeon William Scoville. The man suffered from uncontrolled epilepsy, and it was thought in those days that surgical removal of the hippocampus, a structure embedded in each temporal lobe, would alleviate the distressing disease. H.M. was one of the first and last epileptic patients to undergo such surgery. The effect on his memory was devastating.

True to the amnesiac's form, H.M. could not remember anything for more than ten minutes. If a joke was told to him and he laughed, the same joke was good for the same laugh if it was told just fifteen minutes later. People could be with him for a day at a time, and if they walked out of the room for more than ten minutes, they would have to reintroduce themselves upon returning. More important, an exhaustive series of formal memory tests was carried out on him by Dr. Brenda Milner of the Montreal Neurological Institute. The tests confirmed the qualitative clinical story and gave exact quantitative profiles to his huge abnormality.

Milner and her colleagues were able to propose as a result of their studies that there was a crisp neurological reality to the experimental psychologists' conception of a staged process in memory formation. In short, there was a short-term memory system that received new information, rehearsed it, and then transferred it to long-term memory storage. The brain structure that is heavily involved in this transfer from short-term to long-term storage is the hippocampus. Thus H.M. could remember past events (long-term memory was fine) and could remember new information in the short-term (ten minutes) but could not transfer the information out of short-term into the long-term system. The work was conceptualized as showing that specific brain damage to a particular region (the hippocampus) produced an anterograde amnesia. All events occurring after the injury were not encoded into memory. Thus the brain lesion produced a dysfunction in the brain system that consolidates new information. When all the details are considered, the Milner work established the framework for much of the modern work on amnesia.

Yet it is in the nature of the scientific enterprise to challenge and be challenged by existing hypotheses. New cases or new tests come along that cast different lights on earlier findings. At this moment, memory research is undergoing a revolution that is altering the way many of us think about the problem. And some of the new work came out of findings left dangling by Milner. In particular, she discovered that H.M. could learn how to "mirror-draw," that is, learn how to improve his tracing skills when looking at geometric shapes via a mirror that reversed perception of the shapes.[3] Thus when the hand went to guide a pencil to the left edge of a rectangle, it appeared in the mirror to move to the right. With practice it is easy to learn to adapt to such contrived distortions; and H.M., just like normals, learned to do the task and could maintain his good performance from one day to the next, even though he could not remember having done the task before.

This meant, of course, that information of some kind was

getting into the brain, and that the failure to store it was not total. A very strong motor component was involved in the tasks H.M. originally had to perform, and somehow Milner's finding was left as evidence that memory for motor tasks was different from that for more episodic events. It turns out that it is much more complicated than that.

Another patient, N.A., was tested in California by another group of talented neuropsychologists.[4] Larry Squire and Neal Cohen decided to pursue the issue of skill learning on this patient,[5] who for all practical purposes behaved exactly like H.M. They showed N.A. could learn to mirror read as fast as normals in such tests. An eight- to ten-letter word such as "bedraggle" is presented by mirror reflection very quickly. With practice the time needed to correctly read the word decreases.

Cohen then took his talents East and tested patient H.M. on another kind of cognitive task. He showed that a densely amnesic patient can learn the Tower of Hanoi problem.[6] This is a parlor game that requires the player to figure out how a stack of five concentric rings, each with a different diameter and all placed on one of three pegs, can be moved to another peg such that no larger ring is ever placed on top of a smaller ring during the move. It takes thirty-one moves to carry out the task most efficiently, and each move must be precise or else the correct sequence is broken and the task becomes impossible to do. It is now known that both N.A. and H.M. can perform this task even though they deny at each testing session ever having seen the game before.

Squire and Cohen have proposed that their studies demonstrate there are two kinds of memory we humans learn. One is called "procedural" and the other "declarative." The part of the brain that learns procedures, that is, things such as motor skills, cognitive skills, or strategies like the Tower problem is different from the part of the brain that takes part in declarative learning, which is learning of events. At one level of analysis, their data support the idea of the modular brain. The procedural module is intact but the declarative module is in disrepair.

On a larger scale, the issue that began to surface as more and more people began to study patients with memory disorders was centered on the question of whether these patients did, in fact, consolidate new information. It was argued first by the Oxford group led by Elizabeth Warrington and Larry Weiskrantz that the average amnestic patient failed to access new experiences.[7] The experiences had been recorded but, because of the brain damage, the capacity to gain access to the stored information was impaired. In short, it was becoming apparent that amnestic patients should be defined as people with poor recall but with a capacity to recognize that they had had a particular experience before. Thus, whereas amnestic patients may not be able to recall what ten fruits had been shown them an hour before, they could recognize many of them if placed in view. In such a recognition test a new fruit and an old fruit are shown next to each other and the patient must choose the one he or she had seen before. Since the amnestic patient is able to do this above a chance level, researchers began to wonder why recall was so poor.

It was at about this point in the problem that our laboratory became interested in the issue. In a neurologic clinic it is virtually impossible not to be absorbed by the disorders of memory. They are the single most common presenting problems for the neurologist dealing with behavioral disorders. Memory problems are common in the elderly and manifest in dementia. They appear in alcoholics and as a result of head trauma. Memory disorders are often seen after cardiac arrest. They can occur following strokes, the appearance of brain tumors, and a host of other problems such as herpes simplex encephalitis.

Curiously, however, at this time many of the patient groups tested had been given only a cursory assessment of their memory disorders. It was simply noted, perhaps even measured, where the patients stood relative to age-matched controls. But their particular problems were not carefully analyzed.

One of the reasons for ignoring these patients for study was that some of them had complicated brain lesions and some of them appeared to have none! Since a big part of the cognitive neuroscientist's job is to find the specific brain structures that relate to specific disorders, it was much more appealing to study a patient with a crisp surgical lesion, a known and definable pathology. That obviously made the job much easier. But about ten years ago things started to change on a number of fronts.

First, there were major changes in neuroradiography. Financed in part by the Beatles, the CT scanner was invented by the British. This remarkable device localizes X rays to almost any plane in the head that one is interested in studying in order to detect the presence of pathologic tissue. This means that patients with problems such as memory disorders can now be more clearly defined, neurologically speaking.

Second, experimental psychologists began to shift away from simply considering the short-term to long-term distinction, that is, the problem at the input end of things. More attention was being given to problems of retrieval of information, and how information was internally represented or encoded. (When psychologists change their models, the kinds of questions the brain scientists ask change as well.)

Finally, as one might expect, there emerged the view, mainly espoused by those purely interested in the structure of normal cognition, that any patient could be studied who gave the examiner an interesting dissociation of function. This type of scientist is wholly unconcerned with what brain structures are involved with what functions. Such a view heralds the brain-damaged patient as merely proving that the biologic system honors particular distinctions and therefore, these distinctions must be incorporated into a model of memory processes.

Now there were problems with all of these impulses to open up the study of amnesia. For example, the CT scan records only minimal lesions so that a so-called tight CT-scan correlate is not that at all. There may be hidden damage that the scanner misses.

Thus spurious correlations between a memory disorder and the brain structures responsible for it can occur. Of course, implicit in this observation is the fact that the CT scan can miss real lesions totally.

This and other issues came up when our studies got underway in 1980. Most of them have been carried out by Bruce Volpe and William Hirst. Both of these investigators are inherently unhappy with the status quo on just about everything, and in particular about how the amnesia problem has been viewed. They bring new energy to a field full of creative scientists.

The neurology department at Cornell may be unsurpassed in the quality of its medical care. The chairman, Fred Plum, is an institution in his own time. He is hard-driving, energetic, curious and, most important, completely supportive of our work. The resident staff also assists us in finding subjects.

We had let it be known that we were looking for cases of amnesia. And you have to be careful in the clinic. A few years back an alert resident called me to say that there was a patient up on the ward who was suffering from Huntington's disease, and he felt she was displaying some memory and thought disorders. I gathered my bedside tricks together and went up to see her. Mrs. Levine seemed alert, and I proceeded to give her my bedside exam. Contrary to the resident's perception she looked pretty good; but then on a last-minute hunch, I turned over the hospital menu that listed that morning's breakfast. I said, "Okay, Mrs. Levine, what did you have for breakfast?" She sputtered and said she didn't know, and I began to think we were getting somewhere. I got up, picked up my notes, and told her I would be back after lunch for more formal tests on her memory. She agreed, and as I was about out the door of the four-bed room, she said in no uncertain terms, "Doctor, the menu, I should memorize it?" There was nothing wrong with Mrs. Levine, at least not yet.

Gradually, however, the serious cases began to come our way. First a neurologist from Long Island called with a case. Then one of the professors of neurosurgery called. With each call also came a unique story, both neurologically and psychologically. The trick was to make sense out of it all.

One of the patients, L.K., behaved similarly to H.M. When we first went to test L.K., a group of us drove out in our special van. We were met by L.K.'s lovely wife, who immediately warned us that her husband was not so good on names but was very good on numbers. We all dutifully noted that and proceeded to start testing him. We hadn't been with the patient for five minutes before he too informed us he had a terrible memory for names but he was terrific at numbers. He had managed a deli in his day and was always having to add up the costs of items and as a result became quite good with numbers. Three hours later L.K. had told us that story approximately twenty times, each time with fresh gusto. Finally George Miller, who was beginning to think this was a Bob and Ray routine, said, "How come you have never told us that before?" To which L.K. calmly responded, "You never asked."

After many tests on many patients, a behavioral profile began to emerge. All the patients in a group of eight were markedly impaired on delayed recall of past events. Tests as simple as giving a word list of ten common items could be recalled well after a thirty-second delay. Yet if the examiner waited a little longer, the normal control group performed well, but the amnesiacs were extremely poor at recalling the items.

At the same time—and this is the important point—these patients could recognize the words. In this kind of test there is not the same demand on the patients. Two items are given to each patient, one being from the original list and the other a new item. The test requirement is merely that the patient pick one or the other, even though he or she may verbally deny having seen either. In this "forced choice" kind of test, the amnesiac reveals that, at some level, he or she remembers the original information.

This condition allows for some interesting experiments. The

task becomes to try and understand what went wrong in the initial encoding of the new information that makes it difficult to retrieve. When thinking about this problem it becomes clear that no new piece of information is an isolated element, suspended in time and space, as it were. All experiences have a context and, because we are emotional creatures, a valence of like and dislike is associated with them. The first question Hirst and Volpe asked was whether or not the amnesiac coded new items to be learned in proper temporal sequence.[8] Normally such things are done automatically. Usually if called upon we can recall the morning's events or the week's events in their proper order of occurrence. We don't actively think about coding information in time; we do it automatically. Is the same true for amnesiacs? Are their automatic processes functioning properly?

The experiments I've been describing made it clear that the patients were severely impaired on such tests. In one test design the examiners showed that the patients recognized certain new items that were given to them but could not indicate whether one had occurred before the other. In one form of the test, they simply used everyday news items for their exam. The patient group was a very bright crowd, and most of them read the *New York Times* and watched the evening news. This made them able to take tests on what news events occurred before others. For example, the amnesiacs were asked if the Sadat assassination came before or after the assassination attempt on Ronald Reagan? (Remember, this test was administered in 1981.) They were terrible at it—yet they knew both events had occurred.

Discovering that amnesiacs tend to remember "what" but not "when" argues for the existence of certain superordinate processes being active in human memory. In other words, in my modular view there is a module somewhere in the brain that tags new information and gives it a temporal context. It oversees, that is, is superordinate to the actual recording of information itself. The temporal dating module gives the information a tag. If the module is damaged, the new information does not receive tags.

Clearly such an impairment should greatly affect the normal recall process. Critical cues are not associated with the new information.

There are other examples of how processes that are largely automatic for the normal human seem impaired in the amnesiac. Take, for example, the process of assigning value to new information. The lead for running this experiment came from the fact that amnesic patients tend to have a "hollow," remote quality to their behavior. While they can be highly intelligent and socially aware, there is a marked sense of personal distance. All events are talked about with equal intensity or, more pointedly, lack of intensity. Kathleen Redington and I asked whether these people can form new preferences.[9] The thought was that perhaps the normal brain mechanisms that assign emotional value to new stimuli were not working correctly, thereby making behavior appear flat.

The test we used is a simple one developed by the social psychologist Robert Zajonc. In brief, a series of pictures of human faces or other stimuli are shown to the patient. In the series of pictures, some of the faces are shown more frequently than others. For a normal subject, the faces seen more frequently are better liked, faces seen infrequently are less liked. This finding pleases the advertising industry immeasurably.

When this test is administered to amnesiacs, they show a dramatic inability to form a preference. The amnesiacs cannot respond normally in terms of liking the more frequently viewed faces even though they can indicate which faces had been presented. They seem to have one more automatic process impaired, a process that assigns value to new information. Again, in the modular view, their particular kind of brain damage has affected a system that is normally given over to these duties. When this value assignment system is damaged, the new information receives one less tag, making recall still more difficult.

These automatic processes take real energy to carry out, just as it takes real energy to move an arm and take a breath. They are actual systems or modules in the brain contributing their specific duties to the encoding of new information. If that is true, it is fair to ask the question, where are they in the brain? Most brain scientists act as if they were born and raised in Missouri; they want to be shown the place.

Until very recently that request would be impossible to grant. Detecting brain damage in humans, unless the damage is severe, is not all that easy, and the CT scan can fail the experimentalist in this area, which compounds the problem already mentioned, that a CT-scan lesion merely gives minimal information. Because of these shortcomings the much-heralded CT-scan correlates of behavioral disorders are passing out of style. They aren't precise enough.

Luckily there is a new device in operation at several medical centers, the Positron Emission Tomography Scanner. It is called the PET scanner for short. Like the CT scanner, it takes pictures of the living brain at various levels. Unlike the CT-scanner, however, it shows profiles of how the brain is actually functioning by carefully measuring biologic parameters like the rate of blood flow, cell metabolism, or blood volume delivered to specific areas. This is accomplished by special cameras sensitive to radioactivity which are strategically placed around the head such that they can detect radioactive-labeled compounds that have been injected into or inhaled by the patient. These compounds vary in their chemical nature, as they measure different things. One thing they all have in common, however, is that chemists have made each chemical a positron-emitting compound. This means the compound emits a positron which collides with an electron and is annihilated. This collision creates two gamma rays which then exit from the brain tissue at a 180° angle. The radiation-sensitive camera detects these rays, and they are reported to a large computer which in turn figures out where in the brain that particular physiochemical event occurred. An image is then reconstructed that allows for what amounts to a metabolic map of the living brain. This is the basic idea, and all that we need to know for our present purpose. And the present purpose is that a medical technology now exists that allows for a more sensitive measure of brain disease in the living human. Can it be used to locate our hidden modules?

The answer is most definitely yes, although at this writing the struggle for sure answers has just begun. We started our current studies as the result of a personal exchange I had with one of the world's medical authorities on the matter, Dr. Marcus E. Raichle of Washington University in St. Louis. He is director of the PET scanner there and is a man of enormous talent and vigor. I told him about Volpe's patients suffering from amnesia but who at the same time had no identifiable brain lesion, according to CT-scan analysis. At the time we talked, a great hope for the new technology was that specific cognitive states might be picked up by the machine's analyses. Thus thinking about Keats might activate different brain areas than thinking about the Beatles. That kind of thing is still an open question and a tough problem to solve, but I suggested we try scanning an amnesiac to see if any brain pathology could be detected. He instantly agreed, and within weeks Volpe and his first patient were on a plane to St. Louis.[10]

The interinstitutional marriage worked nicely, largely because of Dr. Raichle's endless generosity, and to date the team has made a number of interesting observations. To begin with, the PET scan unearthed pathologies totally missed by the CT scan. In the patient they studied it was found that the hippocampus was working at a lower than normal metabolic rate. This suggests it was not functioning properly and hence is a possible reason for the patient's memory disorder. It would fit nicely with the famous case, H.M., who had discrete surgical removal of the hippocampus. But there is more.

The old game about giving somebody an answer and having them supply the appropriate question is a daily issue in science. The PET scan is rich with information. Each picture, or slice, of the brain shows relatively detailed metabolic profiles of all kinds of brain structures. Combined with this information is the blood flow information for these same slices. This allows for a comparison at each point whether the blood flow and the underlying neural metabolism are coupled. It makes sense that they are, since it is the blood that brings the oxygen needed for the nerve cells to function. What happens sometimes, however, is that there is a decoupling of the two processes. The blood flow remains high but the metabolism decreases, or vice versa. All of this appears on the scan, and all of it suggests abnormal processes.

It is not so easy to make sense out of all these data. Whereas it is relatively easy to find an abnormality, it is relatively difficult to say that it is the only abnormality present. And, if the object is to try and find a brain lesion correlate of a behavioral disorder, the approach becomes even more problematic. And the added fact that the psychologic theories are becoming more complex, and suggesting the memory system operates using several modules, makes the task for the PET scientists even more challenging. But that they should accept the challenge there can be no doubt, and initial studies are underway. Using new statistical techniques it may be possible to show that other pathologies are identifiable. This suggests that identifying pathologies other than the one I have mentioned and their possible specific locations in the brain could give clues for the brain correlates of the modules handling such processes as temporal coding, affective coding, and attentional mechanisms. It may turn out that attentional mechanisms are the key systems disrupted in memory disorders. Let me explain.

There are other theories in the psychological sciences that are relevant and should be taken into account. In general terms they have to do with what is called "resource allocation," a term meaning that each mental task a human solves in a given moment in time takes a certain amount of the overall set resources a human has to apply to solving problems. Put quite simply, it should come as no surprise to learn we have limited capacities for the processing of new information, and these limitations are tied to biological processes active in the brain. Are the limiting systems mainly in the cortex and associated with language processes or perceptual processes, or are they more general features of the brain that are an integral part of whole brain function? Are they more correctly viewed as sort of the gasoline for the brain cells?

To study this problem we first returned to our split-brain subjects, and Holtzman and I asked ourselves some very simple questions.[11] If one half-brain is working on a problem at a certain level of proficiency, is it influenced by how hard the other half-brain is working? Does the level of difficulty of the problem matter? If the two systems are completely independent, it shouldn't matter. If, however, they are drawing upon certain common resources that are biologically represented in brain structures that each half-brain is still connected to, there ought to be an effect.

And there is a measurable effect. If one half-brain is working on a hard problem, the overall ability of the other half-brain to work is affected more than when the half-brain is working on an easy problem. Here, with this kind of experiment we can begin to see how psychological concepts such as resource allocation can be mapped onto real biological systems. In other words, a problem defined at one level of analysis, such as resources or psychologic energy, might well have a direct biologic correlate in the amount of neural cell-to-cell energy that is available; such energies are limited and set in the brain. From these split-brain studies on resource allocation, it would appear that the whole brain has a set number of resources, that these involve deep structures in the brain, and that they are not divisible. If this were not the case, the split-brain patient would show no interactions between the two hemispheres.

From here it is a short jump to ask whether and how the

coupling between psychological energy and biologic energy might be disrupted in amnesia. Perhaps some of the automatic psychological processes I have been talking about, such as temporal coding of information, try to draw on impaired energy resources in a damaged brain. A general decrease in biologic activity of the brain can exist in patients, represented by an overall decrease in blood flow. One exciting possibility is that such metabolic markers will allow the identification of the specific modules taking part in various aspects of memory function. Untangling this will keep us all busy for quite a while.

CHAPTER 8

Brain Modules and the Unconscious

THERE HAVE BEEN many sources of theories about human behavior; some of the most important ideas have come from Freud. His comprehensive theory of psychodynamics is full of proposals about the underlying causes of our behavior and about our private mental lives. A basic tenet of Freudian theory is that unconscious processes are important in governing behavior. These unconscious processes can reflect attitudes that we do not want to admit we possess. Yet many of our actions are to be explained by these attitudes and by our need to satisfy these processes. Freud in his own way presaged much of modern cognitive theory. He refused to accept the notion of a unified conscious process. He argued, in the early part of this century, for a diverse and compartmentalized mental system.

One can quickly adapt Freud to the theory of modules by changing his concept of "unconscious process" into the idea I present here of "coconscious but nonverbal mental modules." A response tendency, a decision for action on the part of a nonverbal mental module, is not unconscious. It is very conscious, very capable of effecting action. One of its features, that it cannot internally communicate with the dominant hemisphere's language and cognitive system, should not find it being characterized as "unconscious." With that single correction in Freud's formulation, much of what else he claims as important in mental life can be viewed in modern mechanistic terms.

In current experimental psychology, attention has been newly focused on the idea of unconscious processing. Operationally, this means experimental stimuli are administered to subjects, which they are unable to report verbally, but which can influence how they subsequently respond. It is the scientific version of the old subliminal perception phenomenon.

Added to this, of course, is the notion of the automatic processes that were outlined in the discussion on memory phenomena. As new information is stored in our brains, automatic processes assure it is tagged according to when in time it occurred. Imposing temporal order on information is an unconscious process, yet it normally occurs during the awake conscious state.

A few years back when I was on the road lecturing about the idea of mental modules and how I think much of cognitive processing goes on in such modules, a hand was raised in the audience and a meek voice asked, "How many modules are there and what is in them?" I made some sporting response like I hoped one of them was working on the answer to her question but that in fact I didn't know. The question, however, has stayed with me because it is a sign the scientific community is playing its next important game with any investigator, which is, "We'll give you your formulation for the time being, now get on with characterizing the elements in your model." That is the stuff of science, to get on with it and see how much of an initial idea holds up under a variety of conditions.

It is in this context that the paradigms developed in normal psychology are so interesting. Most notable in recent years has been the work of Anthony Marcel at Cambridge University.[1] Many of his studies make use of what is called the lexical-decision task. In the standard use of this test, a word is clearly presented to a subject. Subsequently either a nonword or a related, as opposed to unrelated, word is presented. It has been shown by a great number of investigators that a word related to the first or "primary" word is more quickly classified as a word than is an unrelated word. This "priming" effect is now reported by Marcel to occur even when the usually clearly seen first word is flashed so fast that it is not consciously perceived. If the work holds up, questions can be asked as to how complex the information given to the unconscious processors (read nonverbal mental modules) can be. Do they fatigue? What are the characteristics of their memory? How do the unconscious systems interact? Experiments to answer these questions are currently being carried out.

Our own laboratory work on this important topic is done in a number of ways. One of the most dramatic demonstrations of the existence of unconscious processes affecting seemingly conscious behavior comes from recent studies that Holtzman and I have done on case J.W. The experiment is both simple and revealing.[2]

J.W. is told to fixate a point and either a 1 or a 2 is flashed to the left or right hemisphere. It comes as no surprise that when the number is flashed to the left brain it is named normally. What is intriguing is if J.W.'s left brain knows that the right brain is also only seeing a 1 or a 2, the left brain can accurately name which of the two numbers is flashed to the right brain on the right-brain trials. For a variety of reasons, we know J.W.'s right brain is not doing the talking. It is his disconnected left brain; somehow the right brain is able to set up the correct speech behavior in the left.

It is interesting to consider whether or not the left brain is consciously aware that its left-based speech apparatus possesses the information for the correct response. Could it be the right brain has somehow accessed the left speech/motor system and deposited the correct information for the spoken response, but that the information is not accessible to the left brain's conscious process? The study suggests this is exactly the case. Consider the experiment. Following the flashing of the number 1 or 2 to the right brain, the number 1 or 2 is flashed to the left brain. If the left brain is generally consciously aware of the information, that is, if it is capable of accessing the information in the speech system, it should be able to point to the correct answer. Quite remarkably, it cannot. On this kind of task the left brain performs at chance.

This striking dissociation clearly demonstrates that a conscious system does not have access to all information that governs what is taken to be a conscious response. We do not as yet fully understand how, and through what routes, the right brain is able to set up the left; but that it does so, and in a way that leaves the left brain unconscious of the process, there can be little doubt. Again, a neurologic patient is able to teach us about the multiple levels present in generating our overall sense of personal cognition.

Since my laboratory concentrates overall on the neurologic approach, we find other opportunities to explore such questions. One of them deals with a much-heralded concept called "blindsight." This phenomenon was first reported by a group of British investigators, and has since been reported to have been confirmed by a number of other investigators.[3] Unfortunately we have been unable to confirm its existence, and this being the case, we gain a glimpse of how difficult it is going to be to study isolated brain modules.

Blindsight is a condition found in patients who have suffered from lesions to the cortical visual centers of the brain. The parts of the brain that process visual information are thought to be the occipital lobes located at the back of the skull. Information arrives at these centers by way of the retina which, through an intricate neural-relay network at the retina itself, sends the information first to the lateral geniculate nucleus. This is a laminar (layered) structure in the thalamus, and the first major way station up to the all-important primary visual cortex. I say all-important because it has been thought for years that only the primary visual cortex—that is, the occipital lobes—is able to process visual information. It has been maintained that it exclusively receives the information from the midbrain station, the lateral geniculate nucleus, and then after processing the information sends it along to other cortical regions for further analysis.

According to this simple view of the visual system, when a patient suffers a lesion in the occipital lobe he or she should be blind. The major link between the eye and other brain regions has been cut off by virtue of the lesion. Yet the first clinical "blindsight" reports claimed these patients could see crude information in the huge blind spot. What was so interesting about the nature of their sight was that consciously they claimed they could not see anything. Yet if their hand or eyes were allowed to point to a stimulus presented in the blind field, the hand or the eyes could move to the correct position; hence the term "blindsight." Similar findings were also reported for animals.

In fact, such reports did not violate other known anatomical features of the human or animal visual system. It is now known that the geniculate projects to other cortical areas (see chapter 2). And it turns out that the retina, in addition to sending most of its fibers to the lateral geniculate nucleus, also sends fibers to another midbrain structure called the superior colliculus. This is a good-sized structure that lies just below the occipital lobes. The colliculus in turn sends fibers to other places and it also sends and receives fibers from the occipital lobe above it. Thus, it has been simply reasoned this structure could be a module that is handling such unconsciously generated movements as those seen in the blindsight patient. As a consequence, these patients seem like wonderful candidates for the study of a module in isolation, and that is what we set out to do.

The first task is to find a patient with the proper lesion. We usually hear about candidates at morning report, a meeting held every weekday at 8:30 A.M. The chief resident reports on all admissions to the hospital during the preceding twenty-four hours. Present at the meeting are all of the attending clinical professors. These are the people who do the real neurology of the hospital, that is, the doctors in charge of the sick and needy. Also usually present is the department chairman, Fred Plum, who uses the occasion to keep up on the condition of some forty patients and to teach the current group of residents about neurology and medicine. Practically speaking, every patient admitted to New York Hospital's neurology service gets the added benefit of having his or her doctor hear the opinions of several others on each case.

One morning report was unforgettable. One of the attending neurologists that day was the exceptionally talented Dr. Frank Petito, a man of energy, wit, and medical savvy. It is also important to know that he could have chosen a much more comfortable life; he is somewhat of a financial wizard and his famous father had been a senior vice president at Morgan Stanley. The doctors were reviewing the case of Mr. X, who had a benign brain tumor which had to be removed. At this time, Dr. Plum had the opportunity to make a medical and sociological point of value to the new residents.

"One of the things we have got to do is to let it be more generally known that many kinds of brain tumors are curable. Take my good friend, Mr. X. He thought it was the end for him. We got him in here, diagnosed the tumor, discovered it was benign, and then took it out. After he recovered from surgery, he returned to Wall Street and closed one of the biggest financial deals of our time. Wouldn't you say so, Frank?"

Petito, who knew about the deal (a deal not involving Morgan Stanley) saw his opportunity. He looked up from his notebook and said, "Nickel-dime, Fred, nickel-dime." The interactions are priceless, and everyone benefits.

At another of these meetings Bruce Volpe learned about a case that just fit our needs. A woman, we call her B.H., had suffered a ruptured aneurysm in her right occipital lobe. She was to undergo surgery to fix her leaky artery, and in the course of the surgery, given where the aneurysm was located, parts of the right occipital lobe would have to be sacrificed. Thus portions of the vision in her left visual field would become nonfunctional or blind, but her other visual structures would remain intact and normal. She would show blindsight.

At this point Holtzman and his eye tracker entered the scene. He had been carefully studying the literature of blindsight and had come up with a number of problems with some of the earlier data. It is axiomatic that when one studies the visual system, one must study it carefully. It is perhaps the most carefully studied sensory system and has been so for decades.

Holtzman fired up his computer and his eye tracker.[4] The eye tracker is a highly sensitive device that measures the exact position of the eyes—if not exact, a better one than has ever been measured before in this context. Quite simply, here's how it works, although it is not all that simple. Unbeknown to the subject, an infrared light is projected onto one eye. Infrared light is invisible to the naked eye, but special detectors measure exactly its reflection from different parts of the eye. By comparing the differential reflection, a function performed by the computer, an exact and real-time record of the position of the eye is made.

This is important because Holtzman's task is to specifically limit visual stimuli to only the blind spot produced by the surgical lesion. If light from his stimuli strays over into the normal part of the retina, any claim of visual processing in terms of blindsight is of little interest. With the tracker, if the patient moves his or her eyes such that the stimulus could fall onto the good part of the retina, the computer catches the movement as it begins and immediately turns off the stimulus display. Thus cheating the visual game is aborted.

The actual task was quite simple. Four *X*s arranged in the shape of a square were presented to the blind part of the patient's visual field. Following a certain cue, one of the four was highlighted, and B.H.'s task was to move her eyes to the highlighted *X*. It doesn't get much simpler than that, and of course when the test is presented in her good visual field she performs it flawlessly. Yet, when B.H. tried to do the task when the critical light was presented to her blind visual field, she in fact was unable to perform above chance, this after thousands of trials.

Now it is not a big deal to state that someone cannot in fact see in her blind field. Blind people are blind. But it is a big deal, since there is every reason in the world why, given the actual anatomy of the brain, it could work. After all, B.H. does have these other structures, that is, other modules. Why can't they carry out the task? That is the important question. It is only of secondary interest that so-called blindsight is a field full of experimental error.

We vigorously pursued the matter. Perhaps, we reasoned, the mid-brain module works only when it has normal input from the visual cortex above it. That is, it is devastating for a separate module to function in isolation. Most modules operate as part of a larger interacting system. That a carburetor is different from a piston there can be little doubt. Yet, it would be very difficult to study the functions of the piston when the carburetor wasn't working.

Back to the lab. This time we studied two of our split-brain patients, J.W. and V.P. In these two people, you recall, there was no damage to the visual cortex. As a result, the cortical and subcortical modules are intact. Moreover, it is also a fact that the subcortical modules are interconnected by a neural fiber system. Now since these patients have their cortical systems disconnected, we were poised to study the subcortical interactions and thereby be able to infer what these subcortical modules can do. And Holtzman did just that.

In split-brain fashion, the left brain was unable to verbally report which *X* of the four had been highlighted in the left visual field. Since the left visual field projects to the right disconnected brain that was no surprise. What was surprising was that if the left brain was requested to move the eyes to the *X* in the right visual field that corresponded to the *X* that had stimulated the opposite brain, the eyes moved to the right place! It looks like the subcortical modules can work to carry out this task and can do so outside the conscious control mechanism.

We all rejoiced. The modules can be studied and their varying natural functions can be assessed. In this case, we see how information about spatial location is computed by one such module, and how it can control the eyes and allow for a coordinated response. We also confirm from this experiment that the modules handling spatial information are different from those handling perceptual information. In follow-up experiments it was shown that if, instead of having one of four *X*s be the cue, one of four different geometric symbols was the cue, the interbrain comparison was not possible. The subcortical modules deal only with spatial information, not geometric.

Yet, for the student of the real stuff of cognition, the stuff of language, of perception, of mental images, studies on separating the modules at the cortical level of brain function would be of greatest interest. In order to do that one could imagine that microlesions strategically placed throughout the cortex could effect such disconnections between modules and could thus add confirming evidence to the modular idea.

That high-tech approach need not always be the way to get interesting answers to interesting questions. When it has to be used, it has to be used. But the shrewd use of patients with either special surgical or neurologic status is also important. Such opportunities were made available to us when the neurosurgical team of Wilson and Roberts decided to cut the callosal section, the enormous interbrain connector, in two different stages, at two different times. The first patient to undergo this procedure was J.W. and we were there for all stages of the process.

By cutting the callosum in two sections, one can study the partial transfer phenomenon. Clearly when the callosum is intact, everything presented to the right brain is transferred over to the left brain for verbal analysis. There is little opportunity to see whether or not the en masse transfer is actually multiple modules sending over relevant information. The surgical decision to cut only part of the neural cables permits examination of the possibility of partial transfer of information, that is, whether only some of the modules are able to report to the left brain from the right.

After we got the call from Dartmouth, John Sidtis and I traveled up to Hanover. Sidtis had never seen a surgery and wanted very much to observe the whole medical process, green gowns and all. We, of course, started by carefully testing J.W. in his preoperative state. Words and pictures of all kinds were flashed to each brain and as a normal, intact brain should, the left brain was able to instantly tell us all about visual information presented exclusively to the right. All of his interbrain cables were working. J.W. underwent surgery the next day.

The surgeons decided to section the posterior part of the callosum first. Splitting the posterior region disconnects the part of the visual system that usually transmits to the left brain the actual sensory image of a stimulus that had been presented to the right brain. The two occipital lobes usually can no longer directly communicate their primary sensory information to each other.

Immediately after surgery stimuli such as words or pictures when presented to the right brain elicited a response of limited accuracy.[5] In J.W. the right-brain stimuli produced only a 28 percent rate of accuracy. Over time, however, the scores increased and J.W. became quite good at naming stimuli present to the right brain. What had happened? Had new pathways become active that allowed the sensory information to be transferred to the left brain for interpretation? Or were the remaining uncut callosal connections transferring information from other modules that allowed the left brain to infer what the right-brain stimulus must have been? Perhaps modules that deal with various attributes of the stimulus were still connected to the left brain. Our analysis suggests the latter interpretation to be correct. I'll go through a specific test example that illustrates why we believe this to be the case.

When the word "knight" is flashed to the right hemisphere of a normal patient, the basic sensory information is communicated through callosal neurons to the left hemisphere, and the left speech-dominant hemisphere names the stimulus. In J.W., whose posterior callosum has been sectioned, the raw stimulus information does not appear to be transferring. Instead, the patient's left hemisphere develops a strategy to deal with certain cognitive aspects of the stimulus that do appear to be transferring. Thus J.W.'s left, speaking hemisphere responds as saying, "I have a picture in my mind; I can't say it. Two fighters in a ring, ancient, wearing uniforms and helmets, on horses; they knock each other off. Knights?" The left brain acquires bits of information and then hazards a guess as to what the stimulus must have been.

This idea predicts that when the remaining part of the neural cables connecting the cortical system are sectioned such phenomena should cease. A few weeks later the surgeons completed the section of the fiber system and J.W. lost the ability to name stimuli presented to the right brain. It was as if the separate modules in the right brain that processed cognitive associates of the stimuli then had the remaining interbrain fiber systems unavailable to them.

Another example of how information becomes parceled for the transfer process is as follows. A simple black-and-white line drawing of a traffic light was flashed to the left hemisphere. As J.W. tried to describe what he saw, I asked, "Does it have anything to do with cars?"

"Yes."
"Does it have anything to do with colors?"
"Yes, red, yellow, green . . . Is it a traffic light?"

He then maintained, on subsequent examination, that he had

seen a traffic light in color, even though the picture had been presented in black and white.

These examples strike me as further evidence that mental modules exist, that they are real brain components. It is important to note, however, that any one experiment on any particular patient must always be considered in context. As previously mentioned, J.W. most likely possesses unique capacities in his right hemisphere. That is, we now know that his right brain is one of very few that is capable of processing language stimuli. It has a semantic network that appears to be reflected in a neural network, some connections of which remain to the left brain via the uncut corpus callosum. Yet in a patient S.W., who underwent similar surgery in two stages, there was no fractionation process observed following the cutting of the posterior half of the callosum. Words flashed to his right brain elicited no response whatsoever. Following full callosal surgery, he proved to be without right-hemisphere language.

Clearly, then, the location of various modules varies from person to person. While that point is of tremendous interest in and of itself, it need not dissuade us from considering the results of single-case studies. Rather, the findings on J.W. allow the experimenter to observe a functional decoupling of the information-processing system and demonstrate that such decouplings have an anatomical basis. Brain modularity is not just a psychological concept. Through studies such as this, it becomes clear that modularity has a real anatomical basis. At the same time, however, data from such pathologic-surgical cases should rarely be used to argue that a particular case reflects clues about normal brain organization, that is, about the normal location of specific modules. Getting at that brain architecture will take some time and many more cases. It is a very important point and one we all tend to minimize.

In the continuing search for modularity and its definition in terms of real brain systems, there has recently been a major development. Another imaging device has made its way into medicine, this one based on the principle of nuclear magnetic resonance (NMR). The images the NMR machine can produce are dazzling and give exquisite details of the anatomical structure. It can reveal whether or not a split-brain person has a fully split brain. For twenty-five years I have had to rely on the surgical notes for descriptions of how extensive the callosal surgery had been. Now a postoperative NMR image tells all, and we have completed studies on three of our patients.[6]

Cases J.W. and P.S. prove to be fully split. The image clearly shows that the entire corpus callosum was sectioned. This imaging technique that can verify the surgical reports sets a new standard for reporting split-brain cases, and it also gives rise to new opportunities for study. Consider case V.P.

The NMR on V.P. showed the surgeon had inadvertently spared a very small portion of the posterior corpus callosum and a very small portion of the anterior callosum. These two portions are distant from each other and are involved in different functions—the posterior region is involved in visual functions. Yet V.P., like J.W., does not transfer perceptual information. It would appear there is not enough remaining callosum to subserve such processes. Similarly, the anterior callosum is thought to be involved in the transfer of semantic information in such kinds of cases. Yet V.P. is unable to judge whether or not two words, one presented to the left brain and one presented to the right, are related. At least that's how it seems at first glance.

We have recently discovered that if the words are carefully chosen in a systematic way, the results can be quite different. In the work of Drs. Marta Kutas and Steven Hillyard at the University of California at San Diego, a series of words were tachistoscopically presented, one to each half-brain, in a way that varied as follows: some did not look alike or sound alike, some looked alike but did not sound alike, some sounded alike but did not look alike, and some both sounded alike and looked alike. After seeing each word pair, V.P. had to say whether or not the two words were related. If she could respond above a chance level, it would suggest that her remaining commissures were communicating critical information. The results were fascinating.

On three separate test runs, V.P. scored above chance on only one condition: when the words both looked alike and sounded alike. When the words only looked alike, a condition that would favor use of the posterior callosal fibers, she failed. When they sounded alike, a condition that favored the anterior callosum, she also failed. It was only when the words both looked and sounded alike that enough information was transmitted between the two hemispheres for the correct judgment to be made.

V.P.'s two remaining regions in her corpus callosum seem sufficient to cross-integrate information when both systems are working together and in parallel. In short, different modules have different pathways, and these combine in some way that allows for a correct response even though V.P. is no more aware that she is correct on some trials than she is when she is incorrect on others.

A variety of other studies support the idea that human cognitive structures are organized in terms of mental modules. Consider the question of mental imagery, the ability to produce a seemingly visual representation in the mind's eye of an object or scene. For example, a person is asked to imagine an apple. A beautiful, delicious-looking apple appears in consciousness. It is easy to think that such kinds of visual imagery, which are so vivid for us personally, might be part of the actual visual system of the brain as it is known from neurophysiological and neuroanatomical analysis. We examined this question in the split-brain patients, and to our surprise it does not appear to be the case. Let me explain.

There is a subset of commissure-sectioned patients who are tactually split but not visually split; that is, because of the nature of their surgery, information with respect to touch does not transfer between the two half-brains, whereas visual information does. As a consequence, these kinds of patients can name an object placed out of sight in the right hand, but not an object placed in the left hand. This shows the standard split-brain touch effect. Touch information from the right hand projects to the left brain, and since the left brain contains the speech system in these patients, objects placed in the right hand are easily named. But touch information from the left hand goes to the right brain, and in these patients, because of the callosal section, the information remains isolated in the right brain, leaving the left ignorant as to its nature.

If, however, the object is presented visually in either visual field and therefore to either half-brain, these patients will respond as a normal person responds and describe the object presented. Again that is because the visual connections between the two half-brains are intact and can carry out their normal function. Since that is the case, we would predict that such patients could easily do what is called a visual-tactile match. That is, if an object, say, an apple, were presented visually to either half-brain, either hand should be able to retrieve it by using only touch. The visual system is intact, thereby transmitting the real visual image to the opposite brain. This means either half-brain "sees" the real visual image and therefore can direct the hand it controls to the correct answer. In fact, the patients perform the task with ease, just as predicted.

The stage is now set for a unique experiment.[7] An object is placed in the patient's right hand, and the patient is asked not to name the object aloud but instead to form a mental image. So the patient holds the object in the right hand, and after a moment indicates he or she has an image of the object. I then ask the patient to find the matching object with the left hand. This simple task cannot be done without imagery instruction, since there is a marked disconnection for touch information between the two half-brains. But since a specific instruction has been given to the patient by me to put the tactually perceived object into the visual domain, and since we know the visual system is connected, it is conceivable that the information could now be transferred to the other half-brain, in this case the right brain, and thereby allow the patient to make a correct match.

In test after test on a variety of patients we have been unable to demonstrate transfer through such procedures. This suggests that visual imagery, as it exists in humans, is not a property of the actual visual system but is a computation taking place somewhere else. Mental images are another aspect of our conscious lives that go on in specific modules and, in this case, it would appear the module carrying out the function is disconnected from the right brain, since it proved unable to assist in solving the task with the left hand.

The topic of mental imagery per se has received much attention in recent years from the cognitive sciences. In the studies just described, I have been using mental imagery to investigate questions of brain modularity. Yet many investigators study imagery in and of itself. I wanted to know more about it. I was intrigued with the standard question posed by both students and critics of the topic, namely, is mental imagery something that exists independent of language and semantics? That question is tough to answer but approaches the modularity question from another angle.

One of the pleasures of being advanced in a career is that you frequently have the occasion to ask the right person the exact question you would like an answer to. Not long ago I was walking along a path at Airlie House, a conference center outside of Washington, when I ran into Herb Simon, Nobel laureate, cognitive scientist, and the world's most unassuming man. I wanted to know what he thought about mental imagery, whether it was real and separate from propositional thought, and if so what its properties were likely to be. Herb smiled, sat down on a tree stump, and in the next forty minutes gave a lucid summary of the phenomenon. Basically he answered me with a puzzle. Imagine, he said, a rectangle. Draw a line from the top right-hand corner to the bottom left corner. Now draw a line from the middle of the diagonal to the bottom right corner. Now approximately one third of the distance from the top right corner along the top line, drop a perpendicular line down to the lower edge. How many lines do you intersect? I said two and he said right. My quickness in figuring it out was because I had used mental imagery. Using a system to solve the tough formal propositions would take a very long time.

I was fascinated by mental imagery as an investigative topic, and asked my good friend Edgar Zurif, who works in Boston, if he could arrange an introduction with Steve Kosslyn, one of the wunderkinds of cognitive science who had, more than anybody else, established mental imagery as a real field of study. Kosslyn has critical and incessant energy. He is one of those people who exhausts his friends because of the pace he keeps. He tackles ideas and fights with refreshing enthusiasm and vigor, and he knows his topic like no one else. We met for lunch in New York and I told him I wanted to bring his cognitive technology and ideas into the neurologic setting. He was all for it and a new collaboration was born.

Kosslyn's early studies established the imagery phenomenon as a serious topic for study.[8] Consider one of his experiments, a clever study combining the use of reaction-time measures and imagery processes. He would instruct subjects to think of a dog, say, a Chihuahua, and to imagine they were looking at its nose. Then he would tell them to hit a button as soon as they had scanned along the dog's body and arrived at its tail. That, on the average, took a certain amount of time to do. Then he would tell the subjects to imagine another kind of dog, say, a dachshund, an animal longer than a Chihuahua. Again, they were to imagine they were fixating the nose and as soon as they came to the tail they were to hit a button. Subjects took much longer to respond to this instruction. After all, the dachshund is longer, even in the mind's eye!

The experiments proceed, each more clever than the last and each causing quite a stir in the field. Critics were concerned from the beginning of his work whether or not imagery was an epiphenomenon to the language system itself. Since the language system knows dachshunds are longer than Chihuahuas, perhaps it wouldn't let the response be delivered until a bit later. Clever experimentation brings out clever critics. It is the nature of good science, but in the end Kosslyn has prevailed.

The first experiment was simple.[9] A capital letter such as an *A* is flashed into one half-brain. The task is to think of the lowercase version of the letter in your mind's eye and then say whether or not its printed form would extend above or below a line upon which it is written. Thus an *A* would yield a "no" answer because of the shape of *a,* whereas a *G* would find the subject answering "yes" because of the shape of *g.* Of course, in a test like this, each half-brain has to know the shapes of both versions of all the letters in question. In control tests, the capital letter is flashed. A list of the lowercase letters is in full view of the subject, and the task is to point to the right one. Each half-brain found this easy to do, but only the left brain could make the judgment as to what a lowercase version of a capital letter looked like when generating a private mental image was required. J.W.'s right brain with all its language capacity and with all its superior skills in facial recognition tests was extremely poor at carrying out the task.

There are many fascinating dimensions to this kind of finding, not the least of which is the conclusion that the left brain has a specific module that is specialized for the generation of mental images. The capacity does not seem to be language-based, since J.W.'s right brain possesses a lexicon almost as good as the one on the left. In short, a right brain with language but with no ability to make inference is also incapable of generating visual images. It is one more chapter in the story about how important separate nonlanguage modules of the left brain are in generating our total sense of personal cognition.

Unconscious processes? In some sense, yes. They are everywhere. At the same time, it is now possible to demystify the concept and to see how such intuitive hunches of the past can now be operationalized and subjected to scientific scrutiny. Consciousness in my scheme of brain events becomes the output of the left brain's interpreter and those products are reported and refined by the human language system. The interpreter calls upon an untold number of separate and relatively independent modules for its information. As a result, modern cognitive neuroscience is in a position to study the whole brain and all its processes with equal vigor.

I now leave the realm of human brain science to consider how brain studies instruct us about psychological process. Studying the brain is of interest to me only to the extent that it allows insights into our psychological selves. The physiology of the brain is interesting, but no more so than the physiology of the kidney. It's what the brain does that makes it more intriguing!

CHAPTER 9

Psychological Aspects of Modularity

HUMAN PREJUDICE is a pervasive phenomenon. We all have prejudicial views of matters and they are very much part of our belief system. For the most part they represent the less appealing side of the normal mental operations active in producing our personal beliefs. Prejudice is such a persuasive phenomenon of human behavior that it deserves an explanation. Understanding the mental processes that give rise to beliefs such as prejudices allows us to link up our current understanding about brain mechanisms with what we know about psychological processes.

In Switzerland where I wrote these words, living in an Alpine chalet overlooking one of the world's most idyllic settings, I discovered that even one of the oldest democracies is troubled by the problem of prejudice. The Swiss publically profess that their four ethnic groups speaking different languages—Italian, French, German, and Romansh—live in harmony because of their democratic ideals. Indeed, the country is immaculate, the trains run on time, the food is good, the inexpensive wines are better than those in California, and the landscape is incomparable. It appears that harmony reigns and democracy works. That is what the Swiss say, and it all appears to be true until you live there a couple of months.

In reality the Swiss French barely speak to the Swiss Germans, and neither will speak to the Swiss Italians. The prejudice cuts deep, and in fact the democracy works because there is little interaction among the ethnic groups. The interpersonal understanding of the average Swiss tends not to extend beyond his or her canton. The people living in one canton are all of one ethnic group, and these civilized people have deep prejudices about their neighbors.

We all carry around bizarre beliefs: whites about blacks, blacks about whites, Jews about Arabs, Arabs about Jews, ad infinitum. We are full of prejudices, full of social beliefs upon which we place a continually fluctuating value. Sometimes we have strong feelings about ideas, and at other times we feel less committed to certain views. What is going on? What is the mechanism by which our prejudices, part of our belief system, are continually being manipulated by life's events?

In considering prejudice as an example of a human belief, it is helpful to break the problem down into two related processes. First, it is important to consider how a prejudicial belief is initially established. Second, and more important, it is of interest to understand the mechanism by which it becomes either more deeply ingrained or discarded. Both processes invoke the special properties of the human brain that I have been describing.

One of the major mechanisms that contribute to the formation of human prejudice comes from the incessant left-brain–based capacity to make inference and thereby attribute cause to life's events. When a prejudicial view arises out of these processes it is a serious example of how the human mind can misapply its special gifts and capacities.

Consider the problem. You are a blue person and live in your milieu, incessantly considering your own problems. In walks a green person and begins to compete for your space. It is almost impossible not to attribute some of your problems to this easily identifiable other; thus prejudice can begin. When the differences between social groups are clear, due to color, religion, language, or nationality, the reaction is clear, crisp, and pervasive. When these kinds of cues are not clear, as in modern-day Italy, one of the more homogeneous cultures, the inference-based prejudice system starts in on other more subtle distinctions such as whether or not the other person is from a particular region or town.

There are, of course, a host of other ways prejudicial beliefs are picked up. They can be learned at a mother's knee, on the streets, from the media, or from any other informational source. It is the nature of our species to try to continually persuade others of our views. Accordingly we are constantly besieged with views up for adoption. What is more important to consider is the psychological mechanism by which more or less value is placed on one of these attained beliefs, no matter how it was initially inserted into our overall belief system.

For an explanation of how human prejudices either deepen or disappear in our belief system, I turn again to Festinger's theory of cognitive dissonance, described in chapter 5. His theory fits and has a direct correspondence to my proposed model of brain function. Remember, according to Festinger's theory, when a belief and a behavior are in conflict, the belief must change to conform to the behavior, or the behavior must change to conform to the belief. It is usually the belief that changes. Let me review one of the classic examples as studied by Festinger's colleague Judson Mills.[1] It deals with the problem of cheating.

Many of our beliefs, especially those early in life, are imposed by rote. When we are young, for example, we can roll out the maxims our mothers have taught us. Cheating is bad, cleanliness is good. What happens during the course of our own life is that these views either deepen or are discarded.

In one experiment students were asked to rate how they felt about cheating. Some felt it was a very bad thing to do, others that it wasn't so terrible. Subsequently they were given an exam on which they had to do well. The exam was so structured by the experimenters that it was easy to cheat without being caught. The students were unaware that their behavior was being carefully monitored by psychologists. Not surprisingly, some of the people who thought cheating was bad cheated, and some of those who thought cheating wasn't so bad cheated. After the test, the students were again asked to rate how they felt about cheating.

The results were clear. Of those who initially felt cheating was bad, those who cheated now felt cheating wasn't so bad, and those who did not cheat now really thought cheating was bad. The values of the other group were manipulated in a similar fashion. Of those who initially thought cheating wasn't so bad, those who cheated continued to think it wasn't bad, and those who did not cheat now thought it was bad to cheat.

Here we see how the value of a belief was systematically manipulated by having a behavior be in conflict with a belief. That state of dissonance will not be tolerated by the organism. What has never been clear in dissonance theory, however, is why the organism engages in the behavior that is at odds with a belief in the first place. Why do all the conflicts develop? Enter the answer from our review of brain research. I suggest it is because our brains are organized in terms of independent modules, each capable of action, of carrying out activities that test and retest the beliefs that are being maintained by our dominant left brain's language and cognitive systems. The conflict is produced by a mental module eliciting a behavior, a module that can function independently from the dominant, language-based system of the left half-brain.

The formulation has many other aspects. One implication is that one value of the brain being organized in the way I propose is that it allows for the constant testing and retesting of our beliefs. The responding, exploring human being will have a higher probability of constantly reevaluating his or her beliefs, the sedentary one less so. If the brain were a monolithic system with all modules in complete internal communication, then the value we place on our beliefs would never change. The human culture would be doomed to repeat the cant of its preceding generations in a reflexlike manner. Thus the incessant duel between cognition and behavior so active in the formation of our own beliefs emerges as a very special feature of our species.

Cognitive dissonance theory was proposed over twenty-five years ago and has withstood the test of time—despite minor modifications, qualifications, and even some denunciations. It is a powerful psychological process that is part of all of us. Advances in brain research not only underline its validity but also suggest the behaving human would have little opportunity for an alternative control mechanism. The organism strives for consistency between the beliefs it articulates and its actions. The left dominant interpretive brain tries to bring order and consistency to its mental modules, its mental constituency.

A second important aspect of dissonance theory that must always be honored in order to be effective is that people must freely engage in the behavior that will be dissonant with a prior belief. Most observations that purport to undercut dissonance theory are seriously flawed by excluding free choice, or more accurately the illusion of free choice, as a condition of the experiment. If one is forced at gunpoint to commit a crime, it should not come as a surprise that the person's prior belief in law and order has not been modified. If, however, one is induced to commit a first crime with little outside force, the attitude about such behaviors will most likely change to view the activity as not so bad.

The original work that spelled out these relations came again from Festinger and his colleague Merrill Carlsmith.[2] It was followed up by others, including Arthur Cohen at Yale, who showed how insufficient external justification for engaging in what the researchers called count-attitudinal behavior gave rise to the greatest state of dissonance and hence the greatest attitudinal change. In Cohen's experiment,[3] Yale undergraduates were assigned the task of writing an essay about the actions of the New Haven police force. The undergraduates all highly disapproved of their behavior in breaking up a student riot. They thought the police had behaved most brutally. The students were assigned to four groups. One group was paid ten dollars for the essay, another five dollars, a third one dollar, and one group received only fifty cents. After the essay was written each group was measured on its attitude about the police. The results were clear-cut. The students in the group that had received the least amount of money (external justification for their actions) were the most positive about their attitudes, and the other groups changed their opinions less, with the ten-dollar group barely changing at all.

Experiments such as this illustrate a key parameter in the successful manipulation of beliefs. The studies show that a behavior has to be strongly perceived as freely willed in order for the behavior to be powerful in participating in a belief change. Behaviors easily dismissed as carried out because of external forces do not engage the dissonance reduction process and as a result the belief system remains unthreatened.

Another example concerning the importance of freely willed action comes from an area of psychological research called intrinsic motivation.[4] This is motivation that develops as the result of engaging in behavior perceived to be more or less freely willed. A typical experiment might be as follows. Children are trained in a new body of information or a specific task that requires real effort to learn. One group of children learns under strict behaviorist procedures; rewards are methodically meted out with appropriate effects on acquiring the information. Along with the good behavior of acquiring the information efficiently come more rewards, and so on. Another group of children is introduced to the same new task with the same kind of instruction but is not given rewards for their efforts in the same simplistic quid pro quo way. They too learn the task.

Once the formal lessons are over, the experimenters keep an account of how often the children voluntarily engage in the practice of their new skill. The results are usually unequivocal. The children who learn the skill in the presence of external rewards seldom use it, while the other children go on to enjoy their new ability. The interpretation given to these kinds of experiments is that the children trained with rewards come to consider the new behavior as something to do only to be rewarded. If the teacher reinstates the reward contingency then the behavior will once again appear. Without that contingency, however, the new skill is abandoned until rewards are possible. In short, the children have not assigned an intrinsic worth to the skill itself. Since the skill was not perceived as an act they freely engaged in, it did not become part of their personal beliefs.

The question of freedom is crucial to these investigations of how we establish our motivations and actions, and raises the issue of what a concept of free will means in our modern scientific world. We live in a time in history when most educated people accept the view that all events have their causal antecedents and, intellectually, interpret the world in mechanistic terms. If that is true, why is this psychological parameter of free will so important? Why is the concept of free will, an apparent relic from the past, so crucial to the changing of our personal beliefs?

The most direct and prominent consideration of the question of free will as a construct in a scientific, reductionistic world has come from Donald M. MacKay of England.[5] He rejects the notion that man is not free to choose. His argument stands in contrast to most current assumptions, and he makes the strong claim that our species is personally responsible for its actions, that we do possess free will. His 1967 Eddington lecture states the problem and solution to the dilemma. It represents the major thinking on the issue from a logical point of view, and as such is worth describing in some detail.

MacKay, a physicist, neuroscientist, philosopher, and part-time theologian, accepts the notion that the world is, as he puts it, "mechanical as clockwork." The operating assumption of all scientists is that things exist and happen because an orderly set of prior events occurred that determine the event or action under study. While specifying those prior states is the challenge of most science, that they are specifiable is never challenged. That, of course, is only mostly true. There are phenomena at the atomic and molecular level of matter that some believe are not theoretically knowable because of the problems introduced by trying to measure the phenomena. These issues, which fall into the domain of quantum and statistical mechanics, need not concern us and probably are not relevant to biological processes. The point MacKay makes is that in order to defend free will, it is not necessary to oppose the concept that the universe is as mechanical as clockwork. He develops the idea of "logical indeterminacy," a special feature of an information-processing machine, such as the human brain, that embodies a cognitive agent. His argument can be introduced as follows.

A brain scientist tells me that my wife will eat a bowl of cereal at precisely 7:00 A.M. He knows this, he says, because he has a full account of her brain-cell activity and the cells are programmed so that she will always perform this action at seven. He and I tiptoe around the house and at seven we see my wife start to eat a bowl of cereal.

"See," says the super brain scientist with his electrical recordings, "I can predict her every behavior. She thinks she is acting freely, but she isn't. All is preordained and inevitable for her, if only she knew it." Right? Wrong according to MacKay's analysis. Although my wife's predictable action may have been predictable-for-us, it was not inevitable-for-her. If anyone had said to my wife, "I predict that at seven you are going to eat a bowl of cereal," there would have been nothing to stop her from saying, "No, I'm not."

The brain scientist retorts, "That doesn't negate my view. All I have to do is take her statement into account and my prediction will hold." It is at this point that MacKay feels he wins the argument, and to grasp his point you must understand the distinction between something that is predictable and something that is inevitable.

In order to prove that my wife's future state is inevitable-for-her, the brain scientists would have to prove that it already has one (and only one) specification now, which she would be correct to accept, and mistaken to reject, if only she knew it. This is clearly impossible if the specification implicitly indicates whether or not she accepts it! If the brain scientist does not disclose his prediction to her, he may have a prediction valid for himself and perhaps even the rest of the world. But however he trims up his calculations, he cannot produce a complete specification that will be equally accurate whether or not it is believed by my wife, and so inevitable for her. No prediction of that sort can achieve the status of "universally true." This means there is "logical indeterminancy" about the future states of people's brains; and it is this fact that allows for the concept of free will. It pleases MacKay no end to have articulated this view because, as I say, it has the added benefit of making humans personally responsible for their actions. It is a very clever analysis.

MacKay's analysis, which has been largely accepted as inescapable by the philosophic community, tacitly accepts the assumption of Western civilization that personal consciousness is a product of a unified cognitive system and human action the product of a monolithic brain system. The formulation could, however, be readily adapted to the notion of separate mental modules each capable of action and responses. His argument is not rendered ineffectual by the brain model proposed here, though he does not consider it explicitly. His analysis could confer his "logical indeterminacy" upon any of the mental modules of the brain.

While MacKay's argument seems to put the concept of free will on solid scientific footing, therefore enabling it to be considered a variable in psychological studies, the analysis lacks the psychological reality I am searching for. For, although MacKay's analysis does address the philosophic dimension of the problem of "freedom of action" in a mechanistic universe, it does not deal with the question of why self-produced behaviors have an effect on personal beliefs and externally imposed commands do not. The answer lies somewhere, I think, in the domain that humans—no matter what their intellectual level, no matter what other beliefs they possess—believe unshakably that they are acting freely in 99 percent of their behaviors. The rational point that they usually are not has absolutely no psychological reality. Our immediate experience is too powerfully present in our minds, and it cannot be overridden by a textbook assertion. As a consequence of this overwhelming perception, a behavior initiated by a mental module must be accounted for by the person's belief system. They see no other head to hang it on. In contrast, a behavior induced by external methods has many scapegoats.

Let me return to a clinical example that helps illustrate the power and the need to explain self-produced movements. Our split-brain patient, J.W., is bright and alert. When we place him in the kind of experimental situation described in chapter 5, where both the left and right brains are given a simple task to carry out, the left brain, you will recall, explains the reasons for the two hands' choices. It tells exactly why the right hand is pointing to the card it is touching and then constructs a theory as to why the left hand is responding the way it is. After a few of these trials, J.W. typically becomes agitated. The answer being offered by the left brain is at odds with what the right brain knows. The right brain knows why the hand is pointing to a particular card, and it is not taking the left brain's story lightly. It registers its disapproval through an emotional response. The patient is unhappy and the experiments are stopped.

J.W. is once again briefed on the nature of his surgery, that his right brain has been disconnected from his left, that the left hand may do something sometimes that his left brain cannot truly explain because the hand is really following the dictates of his right hemisphere. He rejoins, "Ah, I got it and I plan to explain to my date next Saturday night the behavior of my left hand. 'I am sorry, dear, you see I have a right brain and a left brain, and. . . .' " We all laugh and the tests continue. They continue after we have given him an explanatory model. Yet the very next trial will see J.W. return intensely to the process of the left brain explaining the actions of the left hand. The feeling is that his left hand is doing something and it must be explained. Explaining self-produced behavior is essential. And, of course, I mean self-produced here in its very special meaning.

The illusion of possessing freedom of action, of having psychological free will, may be the direct result of our brains being built the way they are. A monolithic, completely integrated cognitive system that knew prior to any behavior the reason for it, that always moved from a set of preexamined rules, might well entertain the idea that the world is not only as mechanical as clockwork, but that it is a mere cog, so to speak, in that fixed universe. As a consequence, the illusion of free will would vanish, that is, the illusion of doing things freely. This would render the human mind with a perpetual scapegoat as to why it does what it does, and the consequence of that would be our beliefs would never change as the result of experience. We would be slaves to our past, to what was told to us.

A cognitive system composed of mental modules, each one of which could act independently from the other but all together forming a mental federation, would be most likely to assign to one cognitive system the chore of establishing and maintaining a theory about the federation's actions. Part and parcel of that process would be the necessary concept that the organism was acting freely, that in fact the organism was governable. If the concept of free will were not present, then the overpowering psychological sense of humans ought to be that mental life is chaos, produced at random, and that nothing can be accounted for, least of all inconsistent behavior.

So far I have argued for the existence of psychological processes that are active in the formation of beliefs, and in the assigning of value to those beliefs. The concepts reviewed come out of experimental work, out of laboratory science. The laboratory is my natural habitat and one that will ultimately deliver the valid answers to questions concerning the mechanisms underlying human behavior.

CHAPTER 10

Setting the Human Context: Notes from Prehistory

I HAVE FOUND it possible to keep working at a particular topic only if there are interesting interruptions. If they do not come about naturally, I make them up myself. Around 1980 I was getting restless and this time my new hobby was supplied by Leon Festinger. He had become interested in archaeology, and when he becomes interested in something you somehow find yourself talking to him about this new interest instead of about matters that might have mutually concerned you a week before. When he decides to switch fields he switches, and it is always exciting for those around him.

As the year rolled on, the topic became more and more fascinating. Festinger received a small grant from the Sloan Foundation to pursue his new interests. We traveled to archaeological sites together, discussed our findings, and in the end held different views about what we had learned. I was looking for something useful about the uniqueness of our brains. He was looking at the archaeological record concerning early humans because it was an opportunity to consider first causes; it was a time in human history when things happened very slowly. In more modern times the historical record is not all that helpful at determining causal relations, because any new idea is instantly transmitted throughout the world culture. In prehistory one has sort of a laboratory method of examining, in slow motion, the stages in human evolution; the effects of new ideas on the culture; or, for me, possible brain changes that correlate with major advances in human cognition.

In considering prehistory, it is also possible to look for data or clues to primitive universals that might not only enlighten the hunt for brain or cultural variables to explain human culture, but also possibly shed light on emerging brain mechanisms responsible for left-brain specialized skills. Our slow-motion camera made some interesting observations.

Consider a group of *Homo erectus* fellows sitting around the campfire on the French Riviera, one of their favorite haunts. All day long they had been hunting or scavenging; maybe a few had been making some primitive tools such as existed one million years ago. With *Homo erectus* other options for behavior were absent, largely due to the existing cultural environment. I emphasize cultural environment, because the physical environment was highly differentiated. Yet the existing data suggest to me that *Homo erectus* was unable to seize new opportunities in an extensive way. Contrary to what is commonly said, these early humans strike me as having accomplished very little. As a result, their culture was rather monodimensional. The reason for this lackluster performance, I suggest, was that the brain of *Homo erectus* was not yet capable of easily making inferences of the kind already described. Thus the first step necessary for the establishment of beliefs had not been taken, which in turn suggests the species was not yet ready or able to transcend being in a locked and reflex relation with environmental contingencies. As a result, it did not yet possess the power to carry out any more than simple operations on the environment.

Homo erectus, the species before the Neanderthal man, which was the subspecies in Europe before modern man, was frustratingly slow to produce change in products it could make. The marker that exists in the historical record to support this view is the evidence concerning its use of stone tools. Although *Homo erectus* deserves high marks for being the species that seriously developed the process, for over 1 million years its products were exceptionally monotonous: 1 million years. The quality, variation, and style barely changed from the known onset of the species, which was about 1.5 million years ago, to its demise approximately 100,000 to 300,000 years ago.

Still, this unimaginative behavior of *Homo erectus* must be considered along with other important contributions it made to the history of humans. *Homo erectus* moved about and learned how to keep warm. This early human not only found his way to the south of France, he populated North Africa and parts of southeast Asia. Overall the inventiveness of our genus was beginning to be manifested. By spreading into habitats for which he was not particularly well suited, *Homo erectus* displayed a unique amount of ingenuity. Our ancestors were beginning to show signs that the environment could be controlled for personal improvement. The development of excellent scavenging and hunting skills and the intelligent use of fire are just two indicators that *Homo erectus* was a quantum jump ahead of its predecessor *Homo habilis.*

There are, then, two sides to the *Homo erectus* story. On the one hand his life had a monotonous regularity to it, but on the other he was showing a definite refusal to allow the environment to completely rule his behavior. The hominid was struggling to be in control. The reason he didn't do more, that he experienced what might be called a long, relatively stable cognitive plateau is, I think, traceable to certain identifiable features of his brain. Before describing the brain changes that eventually took place, let's look at the Neanderthal man.

Neanderthal had a much larger brain than *Homo erectus,* and this is often considered very important. In fact, he had a larger brain than that possessed by modern man. Those who think brain size is important in human evolution could make the case, as Professor Gary Lynch of the University of California at Irvine has done, that Neanderthal was more "intelligent" than modern man.[1] When one considers the vast number of human processes Neanderthal man originated, the claim makes some sense. Once the species launched its cultural developments and technological inventions, it could be argued that the species could settle back into a simpler applications mode that did not require as much brain power as Dr. Lynch claims Neanderthal possessed.

At any rate, Neanderthal, who was around for only approximately ninety thousand years, brought life and joy to the monotonous culture of *Homo erectus.* On Neanderthal's arrival, the tools became more sophisticated and also more aesthetically pleasing. Specific tools were made from particular kinds of flint. The soft hammer, made of deer antlers, was invented to shape the stone tools. The skill in making these tools was immense; it was described to us during a visit to the laboratory of Jacques Tixier, one of the world's great lithic technologists.[2]

Leon and I had the pleasure of watching Dr. Tixier make some tools.[3] This remarkable and delightful archaeologist has a full laboratory just outside of Antibes, where he carefully studies prehistoric tool making and where he teaches graduate students this rare art. It is a difficult skill to acquire, one that caused me to doubt my own dexterity. Tixier relieved my anxiety by saying it takes years of hard work and practice to learn how to make the stone tools of Neanderthal.

What struck us about the experience was Tixier's running description about what he was doing. A vast array of maneuvers and decisions must be made when making stone tools: the position of the striking platform and the angle of impact of the hammer (another rock) are just two of these. It suddenly occurred to us that the more or less exponential increase in the quality of the tools made by Neanderthal might reflect the presence of a communicative language; this meant the special brain areas managing these processes which, as we have discovered, are closely associated with inferential capacity, were finally in place for our species. The impact of this development would be enormous. With the advent of such new brain-based skills, the superior techniques of one tool knapper could be communicated to another and would more quickly compound over the years into better ability to make superior tools. I asked Tixier whether he had ever tried to teach someone the skill under a condition where no verbal instructions were given. He had not and shuddered to think how long such a process might take.

In addition to the expansion of tool technology as an indicator of the emergence of a major change in brain processes, there is a fascinating array of other simultaneous developments. Neanderthal learned to use water and began to navigate. It is likely that he migrated from winter to summer homes. This in itself suggests the emergence of a system of mental maps, a process that requires specific brain areas be present and active. Neanderthal also began to decorate himself, which suggests the emergence of a sense of aesthetics. Certain features of the tools, for example, took on an unnecessary aesthetic aspect which went beyond any utility value the tool might have. Finally, Neanderthal began to demonstrate the presence of beliefs, the sine qua non of a brain that supports language. Burial sites have been found, and the particular positioning of bones at these sites suggests to some researchers the existence of some kind of beliefs. Neanderthal is an archaic *Homo sapiens* and one step back from *Homo sapiens sapiens* and from the lightning-fast events that took place with modern man. Since we can't chart a steady upward progression in human accomplishments as real time passed, the question becomes, to what are the changes attributable? There are two main views to consider. The first can be called the bottom-up view; others might call it the sociobiological view. The other view is the top-down view, the notion that things don't start until there is a brain change.

According to the bottom-up view, an organism has a set of genetically controlled response capacities, and these can be appropriately shaped and selected by the organism's habitat.[4] With this view, which arose from a vast number of brilliant and thorough animal studies dealing with the intricate social organizations of various species, such as ants, wolves, and baboons, the social intricacies of their behavior can be neatly explained. These animals live in a dynamic and largely reciprocal relation with their environment because their brain power is not sufficient for any other kind of existence. In short, they are unable to insulate themselves from the environment in any important way. As a result, there can be no doubt the environment plays a powerful and controlling role in selecting the maximal capacities of these subhuman organisms. The bottom-up view undoubtedly explains certain processes in the biologic world. In my opinion, however, the theory is transparently inadequate in explaining human evolution.

According to the top-down view, genetically induced changes in the brain are the key element in human history. Specifically, it was the ever-increasing capacity of the human brain, even of these early hominids, to make inferences that separated them from anything that had existed before in the animal kingdom. The inference capacity, which is the putting together of two novel variables into a hypothesis about possible causes of events, also is the substrate for the formation of beliefs. We have already seen that the capacity to make inference is a property unique to the human brain, and the capacity can most likely be tied to certain specific human-brain systems. Possession of this capacity freed man from the rigid grasp of the environment. Needless to say, the capacity is also very much a double-edged sword.

Consider the power of a system that can make inferences over the kind that cannot.[5] In primitive hominids, inference capacities were limited but nonetheless contributed to the greater cognitive power seen in early man. Say, for example, that *Homo erectus* has stone tool A made out of flint type B. He was always frustrated because the flint splintered too easily. Suddenly he sees a rock come crashing down a hill and notices that it does not break apart. Perhaps *Homo erectus* could infer that a tool made from this material might last longer. The power of inference saved time and short-circuited the always-available but slow-moving method of trial and error. With the appearance of the much more complex brain of Neanderthal, and finally *Homo sapiens sapiens* or modern man, the capacity for inference flourished to reach the point of its current glory where inference has become as automatic as a peripheral neural reflex.

Can any knowledge gained from contemporary brain research that might be applied to interpretation of the archaeological record reveal evidence of evolving inferential systems in early man? The answer is most definitely yes, and it comes out of the work on split-brain patients that demonstrate the left hemisphere's capacity to make inference. This special capacity of left-brain processes also appears to lie in a region coincident with the language areas of the brain. That's the lead. Knowing that, one can analyze data from prehistoric endocasts and try to learn something about the evolution of brain processes supporting inferential processes by examining the more identifiable systems supporting language.

Endocasts are made from the skulls of the various hominids that have been discovered by field archaeologists. They allow us to carry out a volumetric measure of brain size, which is, as I say, a much discussed aspect of archaeological data on human-brain evolution. The problem with the claim that bigger brains are better for cognition has always been that a big brain doesn't necessarily mean better cognition, even when body weight is taken into account. We now know, for example, that the cognitive capacity of a person with half a brain that could weigh as little at 700 cc can be equal to that of someone with a normal brain weighing approximately 1250 cc. With this premise, an argument that the cognitive capacities of someone with a 1000-cc brain (*Homo erectus*) should be different from those of someone with a 1300-cc brain (*Homo sapiens sapiens*) seems moot. Obviously there are differences in internal organization between the brains of the early species of man and these differences are responsible for their different competencies. Evidence for internal organizational differences, however, has seemed unapproachable since only the bony skulls remain; the brains themselves have long since decomposed.

There is, however, a possible approach to this problem. Alexander Marshack, a scholar with a vast knowledge of archaeologic literature, related to me a most intriguing observation that Yves Coppens, a French palaeontologist, had made on human fossils.[6] By carefully reconstructing fossil brains in such a way as to reveal the blood supplies to the lateral surfaces of the brain, Coppens was able to trace the relative distribution of blood supply to key brain areas. These distribution patterns were found by examining the lateral surfaces of the skulls of the various species where the blood vessels make indentation marks. Marshak didn't know what to make of the findings but kindly sent me the article.

The key findings add a fascinating dimension to our knowledge about early human brains. The part of the brain that we now know is crucial for language and inference capacity did not become highly vascularized until *Homo sapiens sapiens,* that is, modern man, had evolved. In the earlier hominids, however, one can see that the appropriate region was gradually becoming more and more vascularized. The importance of this observation is that vascularization is crucial to efficient and productive brain activity. Without a rich blood supply bringing much-needed nutrients to an active brain center, the mental processes represented in that center would be only weakly functional. With no blood supply, as is the case following a cerebral stroke, there is no function. The Coppens data clearly show that the lateral surface of the cerebral hemispheres is heavily vascularized in a brain area called Wernicke's Area. This general zone in the left brain is responsible for major language processes as well as areas that allow for human inference. It is a remarkable correlation.

The importance of the observation lies in the claim that

evolutionary processes for humans are top-down processes. Until this blood vessel supply existed, along with the underlying brain tissue it supports, the kinds of cognitive function we now know these brain areas subserve would most likely not have been possible. The implication is that no amount of environmental influence (positive or negative) on the organism would assist the species in question beyond what its upper limits proved to be. More important, a central change in brain architecture was necessary before human cognitive skills gained the potential to be free from environmental contingencies.

An analogy comes from the modern computer. A computer with configuration A has a finite amount of power. Add another memory card, thereby changing the computer to configuration B, and the power of the machine changes. Once said, it seems reasonable enough, yet it is vastly important. The analogy tells us what has to come first in evolutionary process to produce changes that become socially significant. Those changes must first occur in the brain hardware. Today no one would ask brain-diseased people, those suffering from dementia or mental retardation, to improve on their minimally proficient skills. Nor, therefore, should one be puzzled about the cognitive plateau of *Homo erectus.* His brain was not ready to take the next step. All of this, of course, is reminiscent of the basic features of brain organization that I discussed in chapter 2.

Nothing happens psychologically until the appropriate brain region in the modern developing human brain has become physiologically functional. Before leaving this aspect of prehistory, I should point out that I have been talking about social processes that result from the left hemisphere's capacity to make inference. It is equally important to realize that brain processes, such as changing patterns of vascularization with the correlate change in the underlying neural anatomy, occur, by and large, symmetrically. The right brain is receiving the same kind of attention the left is receiving. What do we know about the corresponding regions of the right brain? Are there specialized processes active here that might be of crucial importance in the evolutionary record as it is presently understood? There are at least some intriguing hints.

Recall that objects of aesthetic quality did not really appear until Neanderthal came along. Aesthetic primitives were realized in stone tools and in the first signs of ornamentation. Then with modern man, aesthetic activity was important—from the famous Lascaux cave to present-day achievements. Does brain science have information on such mechanisms as aesthetics? There are some new leads.

Recall for a moment the findings described in chapter 8 on patients with posterior right-brain disease. They experience disturbances in recognizing unfamiliar faces, discriminating line orientation, and other perceptions. In short, they show some disturbance in their apprehension or evaluation of stimulus material. Could such a lesion also affect aesthetic judgments? Or, for the present context, could aesthetic achievements be managed without a particular brain structure?

We had the opportunity to examine that question in a split-brain patient.[7] We studied V.P. so that we could examine the perceptual and aesthetic life of each of her half-brains independent of influence. Remember that her right brain is dramatically superior to the left in the discrimination of such stimuli as unfamiliar faces. And it is this condition that made her the ideal case for asking the question on aesthetics.

The faces we used for the experiment were pictures from my high school annual, and the attractiveness of the individual faces varied. On a separate independent measure, some faces were clearly closer to ten in attractiveness and some closer to one, on a ten-point scale. We asked each half-brain to rate the attractiveness of the pictures. The results were clear. The right half-brain rated the stimuli, making the same distinction the normals made. The left half-brain, the brain dominant for language and general cognition, was widely uneven in its assessment, unable, as it were, to tell a beauty from a beast.

It would appear that along with the increases in inferential capacity and their implications for quicker, more efficient advances against the mysteries of the environment comes an aesthetic appetite. It is not only that more tools with new kinds of functions were generated. They had to look like something as well. In some sense things not only have to be good at a functional level, they also have to feel good. With a brain structure managing this kind of mental activity, it is no wonder that Neanderthal, along with his more aesthetic tool making, also became fascinated with ornamentation.

It's forty thousand years ago and modern man is looking out over the savanna. His big brain is ready for big things. It is going to take a little time, but this inference-capable human is now prepared to ask bigger questions of the environment, ask for bigger things from it. At this point in time cultural evolution progresses so rapidly that it is almost impossible to detect first causes. Once an idea whose time has come is acted upon, it is difficult to predict and evaluate the multitude of ways it affects a culture and becomes part of the human fabric. It is this problem that makes the historian's task so difficult.

Still, I want to look at one more event during prehistory, circa 8,300 B.C., and attempt to analyze why it happened. It is a very important human event: the formation of large groups. Why did our species choose to move from small groups to large groups? This is an event that I think illustrates the nexus between principles that govern subhuman behaviors and more cognitive principles specific to the human species. Put differently, preference mechanisms, which are an important part of all vertebrates, can be the major motivating factor for triggering a human social behavior. Once a particular behavioral event has occurred, the human makes inferences about possible meaning. These hypotheses become candidates for beliefs which, in turn, can overpower the more primitive preference mechanism. Considering these phenomena, therefore, demonstrates the human connection to the past and also reveals how we depart from the strict constraints of the environment.

The story takes us to modern-day Israel. Festinger was spending his sabbatical in Jerusalem, and while there he organized a conference, this time on early life in the Levant. David Premack canceled at the last minute, so Festinger and I voted to give his ticket to Jeff Holtzman, our mutual student. It was a wonderful trip. Can Jerusalem be anything but wonderful?

Festinger had organized the meeting beautifully. In order for interdisciplinary conferences to work you need a fall guy, someone who will ask provocative questions on both sides. At this meeting it fell to me to play that role, and I must say I did it with a certain panache. I was going splendidly into the last morning when a retired archaeologist was given time to report on the importance of ochre in early cultures. In his heyday this man had done some fine work and had shown how ochre was very important in body markings. The red substance was used in dye, ornamentation, and so on.

The problem was that the old man finished his story and then began again. As he was winding down the repeat performance and it looked as if still another ochre encore was at hand, Festinger leaned over and told me to do something about it. No problem, said I, for I had a number of questions. And because of my phonetic comprehension problem, I launched into an unforgettable discussion.

"Excuse me," I said to the professor, "but what about early use of the substance as a foodstuff?" The group turned toward me. For days they had assumed I knew what I had been talking about, and they then searched their combined scholarly minds for any evidence of it that they may have forgotten. Finally I said, "You know, like for dinner?" The old man looked at me and said, "But how do you prepare it?" I was incredulous. "You boil it. We used to eat it all the time in California. My mom made a terrific okra stew." They nearly had to carry Holtzman out on a stretcher. Festinger, who is occasionally generous in my direction, thought I had hit on a masterful closure to the old man's talk.

We were shown key archaeological digs by our host, the Israeli archaeologist Ofer Bar-Yosef, one of the most respected professors at Hebrew University. Bar-Yosef was ready to delineate some major occurrences of about twelve through eight thousand years ago in the Levant, events he is intimately familiar with since he discovered many of the facts himself. He and his staff have carefully mapped out several sites, some near Jericho in central Israel, some well down into the Sinai. Several of these sites are the remains of a particular culture and people, the Natufians.[8]

The Natufians were a sedentary people, living at about 12,000–10,000 B.C. They built homes and at first formed small groups of about thirty to fifty people. The communities spread from northern Syria south to the Negev. Natufians ate well, dining mainly on gazelle, fallow deer, ibex, and fish. It is clear from their food refuse and their tools that they were also users of wild cereals and pulses of all kinds. In all of their sites archaeologists find mortars and pestles, minute stone tools which were used as barbs or arrowheads, as well as sickle blades and some fish-hooks. Unlike their predecessors, the Natufians appear to have been able to make serious choices about what they would eat on any particular day. The brain's insistence on preferences was being expressed. The pleasures of variety were being discovered by our species.

The descendants of the Natufians, known also as Neolithic farmers, were the first to domesticate the cereals. Tools were being adapted to deal with these new occupations. Storage facilities were built to keep the crops. In short, once the idea of sedentary living took hold, along with the development of all of these specialized activities including the domestication of goats and sheep, which occurred some time afterward, man invented ways to cope with the abundance that resulted from his new ability to adapt the environment to his needs. In this climate of product diversity humans seem to have come up with another major idea, the idea of large groups or villages.

Bar-Yosef explains that about 10,300 years ago a dramatic change in the size of the Natufian campsite occurred. Within a period of 300 years, which in archaeological time amounts to a couple of seconds, the Natufian sites had expanded to accommodate around four hundred or more people. Why this jump in size? At one level there seems to be no need for it. Food is abundant. There is no evidence of hostilities or natural disaster. The small living units of thirty seem completely adequate. Why should this successful group suddenly want to form larger aggregates? The archaeological record cannot answer this question. I think a psychological interpretation of the record offers some distinct possibilities.

Consider the life of the early Natufian prior to the appearance of these new commodities.[9] Although not so monotonous as that of *Homo erectus,* it must still have been fairly boring. The same animal was eaten day after day, year after year—and there are only so many ways to prepare ibex or gazelle. There were no other major foods. The daily activities consisted of making tools for hunting and then hunting the gazelle for dinner. In a climate like this, modern man's known propensity to express preference was not being honored. It would only have been more of the same in a larger group.

Then things started to happen in the Natufian culture. As the result of various discoveries, such as fishing, grain domestication, the selection in killing gazelles, the later domestication of animals, the proliferation of finer tools, the advent of jewelry and probably dozens of other things, the Natufian had a choice. Instead of gazelle again, dinner might be a little fish with cereal. His lady could put on a new necklace; her man could have a fancier spear. It was a bonanza time for our species—it was going to organize itself to take advantage of the new variety of riches. People were going to band together into a larger living unit.

With all of these new specialties more people were needed to produce the products.

In a group of four hundred people, some could be fishermen, some hunters, some farmers, some jewelers. It made sense to give up the simple life and to go to town. There was something to do, to enjoy, to prefer. The brain-based preference system in the human could finally express itself and, I submit, this proved to be a powerful force in the formation of group dynamics, of villages. Once groups formed, of course, new ideas about the social value of other services such as sewers and water supply developed. Indeed, hypotheses generated about the value of living in large groups emerged and were reinforced, yet the initial factor in choosing to live together was related, I think, to the pleasures of allowing the preference system to work.

It was David Premack who articulated the importance of preference as motivation for action.[10] He has studied the process in rats, monkeys, and retarded children. Premack's work shows that a vertebrate does not budge from inactivity unless a less probable response is made contingent on a more probable response. This means it is very difficult to get Johnny to eat lima beans unless he knows ice cream is for dessert.

Are preferences really all that important in the motivation of behavior? In a classic set of experiments on rats, Premack showed both the importance of preference for action and the relative nature of reinforcement. He let one group of rats drink all it wanted. The rats were not, however, given the opportunity to exercise regularly, that is, to run. Another group was given free access to a running wheel but was allowed only a little water, enough to get along. The questions Premack asked were, would the water-sated rat drink more if given the opportunity to run? Would the exercise-fulfilled rat run more if given the opportunity to drink? The answer to both questions was a resounding yes. Anything can be a reinforcer as long as it is the more preferred behavior at the time of test.

Consider another example. This time Premack placed ten

locks of different kinds and shapes in front of a monkey. The monkey displayed a preference for one over the others. That is, a particular monkey would spend more time playing with lock A than with lock B, more with lock B than with lock C, and so on. In short, the monkey demonstrated a preference hierarchy. Premack then examined whether he could influence the amount of time the monkey spent on a particular lock. It turned out to be easy. All he had to do was manipulate the preferences of the monkey. If he wanted to increase the time the monkey spent playing with lock C, all he had to do was make the opportunity to play with the more preferred lock (in this case either lock B or lock A) contingent on playing with lock C. A more probable response reinforces a less probable response and never the other way around.

The importance of preferences for humans is just as great. In humans preferences can be systematically manipulated by the clever psychologist. They can be upgraded, reversed, dissolved. While being based in very old systems in the brain, they play a crucial role in the complex psychological processes that contribute to the construction of human beliefs.

Taking this well-developed psychological principle back to the Natufians permits an explanation. Powerful energies were unleashed by the appearance of a variety of commodities for human consumption. Prior to their appearance the motivating value of possessing a preference hierarchy remained unactivated because of the limited availability of goods. The small group was sufficient. With the advent of more commodities, which allowed the preference system to function, the small group did not prove sufficiently resourceful to supply the goods for these preferences. The large groups did, and when they formed, motivated by rather primitive impulses common to all species, they inadvertently began a new era for humans. This new social climate catalyzed the formation of seemingly endless beliefs and social institutions.

Modern humans make inferences reflexively and about almost everything. They make inferences by correlating two events that take place contiguously. The average mind takes great pleasure in building theories based on these surface correlations. Only a trained and educated mind learns to inhibit this reflex and sometimes look for hidden or other causes. As we all know, it is a very active process because the making of surface correlations is a lot easier and is usually amusing.

Thinking, even thinking simply, is unique to man and is what enabled him to adapt and control parts of his environment to his own purposes. Thinking clearly about complex variables is also unique to man, but it is hard work. Man engages in this process very rarely. In order to do it he needs to be aware of accumulated information. Without accumulated information, he has only the more elementary power of thinking simply. Information did not accumulate during prehistorical times and that is why things took so long to develop for early man. The culture was not offering to the inferential brain enough data to move it along.

Henri Frankfort argues that, contrary to popular views that prehistoric man was prelogical, early man's thought processes were quite clear.[11] Frankfort makes the profound point that ancient man lived on the thin edge of the present. There was no history, no recorded experience. There was nothing but his subjective reaction to immediate events. In a situation like that, human cultural advances would proceed slowly indeed.

Perhaps, however, such a climate wasn't all bad. With no recorded history, there was little chance one human could misunderstand the interpretation of life's data offered by his neighbor. As a consequence, interpersonal hostilities would be less.

Consistent with this data, there is in the record of prehistory virtually no evidence of assault by one human being upon another. Homicide may have been as rare as ducks killing each other. If all members of the species have available to them the same data, then it would not be too surprising to think they came up with the same inferences and developed the same beliefs about the nature of the world. As a result, conflicts were rare.

With the advent of groups, however, hostilities became common. Full-scale wars occurred after man had developed the opportunity to have his preferences entertained by the growing, diverse environment he had constructed for himself. They also came at a time, more or less, when human behavior was beginning to be recorded. It is hard to imagine a more perfect climate for the human inference system to develop and to generate beliefs about the nature of culture. These times represent the turbulent beginning of a complex human culture. Instead of living only in the present, it was possible to interpret what others had experienced in the past. With this, of course, came the beginnings of interpretive history. Again, it was the perfect setting for the widespread launching of beliefs, of different views about the world.

In summary, the view is that the archaeological record is suggesting specific brain areas evolved to carry out specific functions that in turn produced new capacities for our species. These capabilities, such as inference and aesthetics, are manifestly present in *Homo sapiens sapiens.* Their origins can be traced all the way back to *Homo erectus,* perhaps further. The ensuing cognitive skills came slowly, and in prehistory early man was capable of making more associative responses than inferential leaps. Once inference was possible, however, modern man was born into and doomed to a most difficult way to live. The inferential capacity led to the formation of beliefs, not only about his own behavior but also about the past and present behavior of others within his group. Such mental activities in turn begin the process of decoupling man from the influence of environmental forces.

CHAPTER 11

On the Inevitability of Religious Beliefs

RELIGIOUS BEHAVIOR for most people expresses an intense, serious belief. The most serious believers are those who spend a great amount of time studying the tenets and claims of their particular belief and who practice the rules of their faith. Even Sunday Christians or Friday Moslems are believers, part of the large pack that follows the true believers. In Qum, at this writing, some fourteen thousand mullahs spend from seven to thirty-five years studying the mysteries of Islam so that in their remaining years they may advise Iranians. They are true believers.

Forces from both the environment and the self contribute to the formation of strong religious beliefs. In order for strong beliefs to be inculcated, the religion in question must initially exercise strong control over neophytes. Its promulgators try to create an environment that minimizes situations where a religious tenet can be broken. Allowing the occurrence of a behavior that conflicts with the tenets of the belief makes inroads on the belief. For the true believer, things like sleeping with Susy outside of wedlock or drinking Scotch must be very tightly controlled. The discovery that one's head does not instantly fall off at the will of God, or Allah, or whomever, following a transgression of a group's beliefs, would be disturbing information to the young believer. Those opportunities for the multiple mental system to work must be forbidden.

In religious beliefs, as with any other belief, we again see the left-brain interpreter seeking an explanation for a series of life experiences. Just as it is charged with delivering a running explanation of the behaviors of all of our independent modules, it is similarly charged with explaining real-life events and circumstances existing in the culture. It is seeking consistency, and the left-brain interpreter module, linked as it is to the special human inference system, works hard to construct theories about the causes of perceived events. That our brains accept the theories this system comes up with is also of interest.

But how did the idea of religion start? Why did our species generate the idea of deities? The nature and origins of religious beliefs has an intriguing and, I think, interpretable history that underscores the centrality of the brain-based psychological mechanism I have been describing. I will argue that religious beliefs were inevitable and had to start once the left-brain interpreter was fully in place and reflexively active in seeking consistency and understanding. Explanations were generated and institutions created to manage and deal with the issues of human existence and cosmic origin. Once launched, such institutions, given their intense coercive power, have a way of staying.

Alternative views like the ones now readily available from modern science and those made available by Aristotle have played and continue to play a subordinate role to beliefs involving revealed truths. And, in an effort to explain this fact, I will also argue that the acceptance of these not-of-this-world beliefs is due to another special capacity of the human brain, the capacity for magical thinking. Let me explain.

There is a region of the human brain that, when tampered with, causes profound changes in the human psyche. A lesion in that region, which can come about for a number of reasons, tends to cause a change in three behaviors. This "temporal lobe syndrome" was first described in detail by the late Norman

Geschwind of Harvard Medical School.[1] I would have been most skeptical of his account if I had not seen a case that exactly matched his description. This syndrome now has been reported several times. In its basic form, the brain injury causes a deepening of religious conviction, a desire to write extensively (hypergraphia), and the performance of bizarre sexual activity.[2] There is no a priori reason I know of why affecting one of these behaviors ought to affect the other two!

The reality of the syndrome is not amusing. Of interest here is the religious behavior aspect of the syndrome. Not only is conviction deepened, but the form it takes becomes erratic and the person switches from one belief to another rapidly and without apparent cause. The brain process that allows for nonrational and magical interpretations of events that are usually implicit in stories of religious creation is readier than ever. It seemingly doesn't matter which belief is plugged into this process. In a way, the brain lesion frees the patients from their personal histories and prepares them for any set of beliefs. These clinical phenomena suggest that a dynamic equilibrium can be set up in the brain between systems that generate hypotheses and systems that accept such explanations as meeting rational criteria. The normal state allows for a certain degree of nonrational and magical beliefs. The diseased and disinhibited state so lowers the criteria for acceptance that rapidly accepting and changing beliefs become the rule.

If there are brain networks in our modern brains that do tilt us toward magical beliefs, it would follow that there should be evidence for religious behavior in primitive humans, at least in all humans who possessed the same brains as those we possess. That means we could examine the prehistorical record back to approximately forty to sixty thousand years ago and, if clever enough, find evidence of religious practice. It turns out that the record is replete with such evidence.

The evidence for religious practice prior to 3,000 B.C. has to be inferred from the unwritten archaeological record. In the main, the data come from the variety of burial practices that can be traced back at least forty thousand years, and some archaeologists maintain that even earlier evidence exists.[3] Most of the data take the form of the odd positioning of the bones of the various unearthed human skeletons. Other, more indirect evidence is found in the cave paintings of southern France. These drawings demonstrated that seventeen thousand years ago man could draw with skill, showing such dimensional ability as interposition, shadowing, and other artistic techniques. Yet these skills that gave rise to perception of depth and form were applied only to animals. Human representations in these drawings were pathetic in comparison and for the most part were simple stick figures.[4]

Some drawings showed figures half human and half animal. Historians have theorized that these data suggest a religious devotion. They theorize that, for some unknown reason, depicting man on a tablet or an enduring medium was taboo.

Whatever the case, there is much archaeological data to suggest that early humans were engaged in practices that had no obvious utilitarian value. Something magical had to be happening in their thinking that motivated them to these kinds of activities. They believed something about the uniqueness of their species.

It wasn't until the written record came into existence that it became possible to track what the mental antecedents to human religion as we now know it might have been. Remember, these were brains like yours and mine dealing with the data presented by that environment. The human brain's inference-making device wanted badly to come up with a theory to rationalize activities into a parsimonious reality. As is true of our own time, the brain wanted to find consistency in an otherwise uninterpretable set of events. And, contrary to current assumptions, my reading of history suggests that the human brain-based system ultimately strived for a form of monotheism, that being the most parsimonious view of creation. The reason for holding this view will soon be obvious.

Consider the world ten thousand years ago. Throughout the entire world there were at most only ten million people. Of these, half were under the age of ten and the oldest and wisest in the village was typically only thirty. There is no reason in the world not to think that this inference-capable human did not experience a dash of existential despair. "What," he might ask, feasting on roast gazelle, "does it all mean?" His dilemma must have been grave. Everything this organism did had meaning. If he didn't get up and go hunt, he didn't eat. If he didn't build a hut, he was cold. If he didn't domesticate wild grain, his diet was boring. Finally he asked, "I know why I do all those things, but why am I here?"

The first signs of what this process yielded don't appear, as I said, until about 3,000 B.C. From that time written records abound, and interestingly for our purposes they exist in different cultural settings. That gives us the opportunity to check out some armchair hypotheses about what ancient man's thought might have been about.

My model is based on the assumption that something about the species (a property of our brains) inclines it to yield to a belief in a greater order than that perceived around it. The psychological mechanism is through the inference system, and it is realized by the process of attribution and by the human brain's capacity to accept magical beliefs.

Picture ancient man questioning the meaning of life, and assume that the brain can be given over to magical thinking. It goes without saying that this early human is going to look to the immediate environment for ideas about supernatural processes. Environment A should yield one theory of what a god should look like, and environment B, if it is truly different, ought to produce quite another theory. I want to argue that the historical record supports this hypothesis. The Egyptian view of creation is quite different from the Mesopotamian view. Both came about at roughly the same time and both were generated by the same human brain that is with us today. The only thing that was different was the brain's physical environment. The late John Wilson of the University of Chicago has described these differences in fascinating detail.[5]

The Egyptians saw the world as a very orderly place and their role in it as supreme. They lived in a highly structured environment, the Nile valley. Every morning the sun rose in the East and set in the West. All the Egyptian had to do to control his environment was to take a seed, plant it in the ground, sprinkle a little Nile water and rich silt on it, and watch it flourish. Things were very orderly indeed.

It is not surprising that as a consequence the ancient Egyptians inferred that the sun had special powers. They came to worship the sun and generated the idea of a sun-god, Re. The sun had to be the reason for their good fortune. The sun was male and by all legends was considered the first divine king of Egypt. This god was so primary, so great, he could divide himself into separate entities, each responsible for a single aspect of life. Thus there was Re-Atum, the creator god of Heliopolis; there was Re-Harakhte, the god of the eastern horizon—a very special direction for Egyptians, since that is where the sun appeared for each new day. Even local communities were able to use this god. For some he became Sobek-Re, a crocodile god; for others, Khnum-Re, a ram god; and so on. It is of interest that Re himself was depicted as wearing a beard and possessing two disks over his head.

But establishing that the Egyptians put great importance on the sun and gave it divine status does not answer the question of why everything exists. Their magical thinking needed a creator. That was easily solved. Re-Atum, the creator god, was sent to begin life from the primeval waters of Nun on a little mound of dirt in the town of Hermopolis, the kind of mound that is always deposited by the Nile during the yearly floods. When the Nile recedes, these rich mounds of new soil generate the new season's fertile surrounds. Thus the point of origin for the creator god. The Egyptians' religious beliefs came straight out of their everyday experiences with the environment.

This god, Re-Atum, also needed assistance and so other constructs were developed. How did Re-Atum, who was self-created, get all the chores of his kingdom done? Atum itself means "what is finished, completed, perfected." With that posture, Atum clearly needed a staff. For example, how did the heavens and earth separate? Well, the goddess, Shu, took care of that. She was the goddess of the air and held up the heavens. In some accounts she was helped with pillars. Other chores required other gods and all of these become part of the story. The point to keep in mind, however, is that there was, in a sense, only one supreme god—Re. The other gods were really and truly secondary characters in this formulation of creation. And the plot thickens.

The physical instantiation of all of these gods, from Re down to the more junior gods, was becoming less appealing to the citizens living in Memphis. Intellectually things were a little disorderly, so a concept was developed that explained matters of creation more neatly. A new supreme god was invented not only to explain the activities of Re but also as an expression of the key idea that there is but one force behind all of these activities. Enter the god Ptah. The source of this remarkable knowledge about Ptah's origin is a stone tablet that is in the British Museum.

Ptah is equated with Nun, the primeval waters out of which Re-Atum emerged. Having given Ptah this status, the stone goes on to say that Ptah, because he is the "heart and tongue," which means mind and speech, of the one creator Ptah, created Re and his ennead of gods. Ptah wants more. Not only does he transmit all power to gods, he wants to be the power behind everything that exists. The tablet says "It has come to pass that the heart and tongue control {every} member (of the body) by teaching that he (Ptah) is throughout every body (in the form of the heart) and throughout every mouth (in the form of the tongue), of all gods, of all men, of {all} animals, of all creeping things, and of what (ever) lives, by (Ptah's) thinking (as the heart) and commanding (as the tongue) anything that he wishes." Power is thus centralized and the Egyptians have opted for a much more parsimonious description of events. As has been pointed out by others, this formulation has all the earmarks of the triune god of the New Testament. Ptah is the heart and tongue. He has ideas from the heart and then gives commands through the tongue. Compare that to "In the beginning was the Word, and the Word was with God, and the Word was God."

The point here is that the orderly environment of the Nile valley generated a more or less orderly concept of creation. From Nun to Ptah there was a striving for a kind of monotheism, and that simplicity reflected the simplicity of life as the Egyptian experienced it. It also prepares us for the realization that the idea of monotheism probably did not come de novo from the Hebrews. It certainly is implicit in the Egyptian experience, even though it was never formally realized.

Let us now examine how the Mesopotamians constructed their theories of creation, of religion. Life was different then in what is now modern-day Iraq. In Egypt the fertile Nile had produced its tranquil view of life; man was central, powerful, and the gods supplied the continuing resources for a bountiful life. In Mesopotamia, there was no such good fortune.

Unlike the Nile, the Tigris and Euphrates rivers can break the spirit of a man. They flood unexpectedly. Scorching winds there produce dust storms of unwieldy magnitude. Torrential rains turn the land into mud and paralyze movement of every kind. It is a place of infinitely complex environmental contingencies. And to communicate what it must have been like, how difficult it must have been then to generate a reasonable theory of nature, let me digress a moment for a look at how a modern-day institution works: medical practice. The variables active in keeping someone well are indefinable. As my physician father put it, "It is not why people die that is a mystery. It's why they live."

A medical doctor is faced with a patient who has a disease of supposedly identifiable origins. The doctor diagnoses, prescribes, and waits to see if the proposed solution takes effect. If it does, the doctor files the diagnosis away in his mind with a theory for a cure. Enter the next patient with supposedly the same disease. The physician tries the last successful cure. It is applied, but this time it doesn't work. He keeps on trying until something *does* work. That is also filed away, and then tends to be the next applied cure, which may or may not work.

In still another situation, the doctor proposes a cure that he formulates on the basis of some spurious data in the patient's history. That also goes into the doctor's personal bank of clinical wisdom. The result of this ad hoc thought process can be a lot of ill-formed theories about medicine. But the reason for it is no mystery. The modern medic is not unlike the Mesopotamian. He is trying to function in a stormy and diverse environment he frequently has little control over; there are too many variables. I suggest in such situations people adopt similar coping measures or philosophies to deal with their problems.

In modern medicine, physicians generally adopt an authoritarian strategy to deal with the world. They realize all of their privately held theories need an arbiter. They realize their professional group needs a policy. August bodies are formed, and while individual positions are argued vehemently (and privately), a general public policy is usually announced. The ad hoc nature of much of the enterprise is covered over. In general terms theories to explain the diverse events abound, and the need for a central authority becomes apparent.

Like the doctor, the Mesopotamians inferred the existence of a diverse set of gods to describe the difficult patient, which in their case was the unpredictable environment. They were also the first people in human history to set up authorities to deal with the chaos: a strong family structure and the city-state system. Let us consider those stormy times.

In the first place, the Mesopotamians didn't concern themselves with the importance of the sun.[6] That was a backdrop to other far more problematic entities. The god most highly valued was Anu, the god of the sky. Most of the problems came from above, and the sky enveloped all. Right behind Anu in the Mesopotamians' concern were the gods of storms, rain, dust, and wind. The god who supervised these elements was called Enlil. Then came the elements from the earth; the gods Enki and Ninhursaga were in charge here.

The key to Mesopotamian myths of creation and of their gods is the inordinate concern for details. While some of their dominant, primary myths have god pairs coming out of the water, probably at the fertile junction of the Tigris and Euphrates, to produce god offspring such as Anu, the really serious myths concern the god of storms, Enki.

Enki's story is endlessly detailed and represents an effort to explain the psychological character of complex human relations. This is a first and is a theory based on the very different cultural environment of Mesopotamia, a culture that didn't consider man the center of the universe. How could it? Everything man tried to do was undercut because of his position in an unpredictable environment. With such an environment to live in, it follows from all I have said that people were going to come up with more theories as they tried to explain and correlate what caused what. There were more theories because each citizen was having different experiences as a result of the diverse environment, and each experience had its own explanation. With this rich diversity came the need for details. Two people meet and discuss the same calamity but each has a different theory. In order to explain this difference, they come up with the details. No such problem existed in Egypt. Everyone there had the same experiences, and one set of interpretations could explain the fact that the sun always rose in the east and set in the west.

The view I am proposing is that early humans, just like modern humans, possessed a capacity to entertain magical beliefs. These beliefs came from personal experiences, which in turn differed widely depending on the climate and environment in which people lived. Given that people were prepared to ask questions about origins, the day-to-day data from which they were to draw their inferences varied enormously; therefore, so did the nature of their ideas of creation.

For the predictable world of the Egyptian, man was central, god was good, and there was a strong tendency to believe in one main god. At least that is how they finally hammered out their view. Their lives blossomed and their notions of how to organize the universe were expansive.

In the unpredictable world of Mesopotamia, our species had a chance to develop a much more theory-laden view of the world. Nothing seemed to follow from antecedents except by developing elaborate theories. Everything took on a psychologic character and the emphasis was on details. Only in the details could the possible real correlates of first causes be found.

In both cases, however, the human brain's unique capacity and insistence on making inferences from observed events is responsible for the two different constructions of creation theory and, finally, personal beliefs. Give the inference system orderly data (Egypt) and it generates an orderly universe. Give it disorderly data, and the inference system constructs a vastly more complex notion of creation—one that emphasizes the helplessness of man. Yet in both cultures a close examination of the hierarchy of imagined gods reveals that the inference system would not let go of the idea of one supreme God. In Egypt it was Ptah and in Mesopotamia it was Anu. The human inference system wanted parsimony.

Surely, from this quick review of brilliant scholarly history of others, such as the late John Wilson, one begins to see glimmers of the underlying psychological mechanisms involved in religious belief. Just as the split-brain patient seeks a unified theory to explain his or her own behavior, and just as normal humans do the same for understanding personal actions, humans seek a parsimonious and unified explanation for the logic governing worldly matters. Consistent with this view is the claim that so-called polytheism is in fact an early form of monotheism. The human brain seeks order, reflexively, even in religious belief.

Try as I might, I find it difficult to read ancient history and believe the polytheistic assumption. In both Egypt and Mesopotamia, there is a very definite hierarchy of gods. In fact, I doubt there has ever been anything like a nonhierarchical organization in the history of man. The politburo of the Soviet Union has a chairman. Anu was the final arbiter for the Mesopotamians. The same is true for the Egyptians and for every example of successful organization in existence. It has to be this way. It is in the nature of decision processing.

Even today elements of polytheism are present in the monotheisms of *Homo sapiens sapiens.* Catholics can pray to a saint, to the Virgin Mary, to the Holy Spirit. These religious elements can intercede with the Lord on behalf of the client just as Khnum-Re could work on Re-Atum.

Again my point is that we are looking at a universal psychological mechanism at work here that has always taken more or less the same form. As the human hypotheses gradually evolved about first causes, it became apparent that having several gods within a culture was unwieldy. Many of these gods no doubt developed rather independently within the culture as the separate diagnoses of individual members of that society. But as the culture moved forward they were gradually collated into pantheons or assemblies, and a supreme senior god was identified. Clearly the Egyptians moved ahead from this with Ptah and tried to rewrite their own history in one true voice. A society cannot have ten presidents or ten gods. The idea has to be condensed and the concept made orderly. In short, our species was never really without the concept of monotheism.

That is not to say the concept didn't need work. It clearly did, and Moses seems to have played a major role. For forty years he isolated himself from the Egyptians on the one hand and from the Syrians on the other. The idea Moses finally announced grew out of a very complex history. His god had certain key features. First of all there was going to be no room for idolatry. There were to be no graven images. Thus God says to Moses, "I am what I am," which Professor Albright says means, "He causes to be," or "He causes to be what comes into existence." The idea is one of the creator of all things, of having no family, living in no special place; it is slightly anthropomorphic but more aniconic. God should be kind, he should like children, and so on. Moses addressed these issues, and Judeo-Christian tradition was launched. When you think about it, it is a story every bit as astounding as Joseph Smith's.

Meanwhile in Greece, our species had not yet caught up to the rank monotheism of Moses. It was still dealing with the existential question, the same way as the Egyptians and Mesopotamians were. Gods were being constructed for everything. There was an Artemis of Brauron, of Aegina, of you name it. Minor gods helped the fisherman, the baker, or the candlestick maker; others dealt with hope and charity. It all became too much and, gradually, as with earlier societies, the Greeks moved toward a syncretism. Zeus was the head god, the final arbiter.

Somehow the god system wasn't as richly received. Not long after their full-blown establishment, the Greek philosophers attacked the notion. In Greece a few men put reason before belief and put forward the idea of monotheism because it was the most logical. As Professor George Boas points out, in the sixth century B.C. the philosopher Xenophanes ridiculed the notion of multiple gods.[7] He promoted the idea of one god, a god with many features of Moses's God.

Boas gives another example of philosophic theology from Cleanthes' "Hymn to Zeus." The poem is remarkable in the intensity of its mood and in Zeus's rank similarity to the god of the prophets.

Zeus, ruler of immortals, you of many names, ever omnipotent,
Zeus, ruler of nature, governing all by law,
Hail! for it is man's duty to address himself to you,
For we are your children, being, as it chances, the sole image of one,

Whatsoever mortals live and move about the earth,
Wherefore to you shall I sing hymns and your power shall I forever celebrate.
You and none other does the cosmos, circling round this earth, obey
Whithersoever you lead, and willingly is it led by you.
These have you as servants in your invincible hands,
The forked lightning, fiery, ever-living;
When it strikes, all nature trembles.
By it you guide the universal Logos, which pervades all things,
Mingling with both the greater and lesser stars;
As you have been and are supreme ruler of them all.
Nor is any deed done on earth against your will, O Lord,
Either in the high and divine heaven or on the sea,
Save that which evilmongers do in their madness.
But you know how also to render the even odd,
And to bring order into the unordered, and the displeasing is pleasing in your sight.
For so have you brought all things into unity, good with evil,
That the universal Logos, ever-being, has become one.
When the evil flee from it, they become
Miserable, and those of good men who always yearn for the possession of wealth
Neither see the common law of God nor listen to it;
But evildoers again and again strive indecently for something else,
Some possessed by passionate zeal for fame,
Some turned to craftiness in complete disorder,
And others to the shameless and voluptuous deeds of the body,
Hastening in all ways to become the opposite of the good.
But Zeus, giver of all gifts, shrouded with dark clouds, you of the bright lightning,
Free men from endless misery,
Which you, Father, may expel from their souls, and give us the power
To be governed by your mind, trusting in which you govern all things with justice,
To the end that honoring you, we may share in your honor,
Hymning your works continually, as it is fitting
For a mortal, since there is no better prize for men
Or for gods, than ever to celebrate the universal law in justice.[8]

But there were problems with the theologic and metaphysical gods of the Greeks. They did not make demands of man. All of the Greek monotheists believed that the purpose of life was to achieve self-sufficiency, to arrive at a state of autarchy. Plato, Aristotle, the Stoics, all saw it happening in different ways, but that was the gist. Since their conception of the logic of the universe was to be found in logic itself, it follows that the chore of life would be to establish independence from all frailties of the heart and vicissitudes of society.

Needless to say, the problems created by these different views of monotheism and their implications still pursue students of these issues. What should be clear is that early man turned his mind toward matters of first cause; his ideas evolved from his personal experience, which in turn came from his environment. Although these produced interesting differences in the style and content of the theories, it is my contention that the same overall commonality of data took the form of a brain-based inference system, and the progression of ideas was remarkably the same. It makes human history understandable, not bizarre.

As a consequence of this analysis, it seems to me we have a rationale for explaining why religious beliefs are so easily accepted in the atomic age. Underlying the surface appearance of differences, beliefs all share a common form, and that form is and has been always totally acceptable to human thought. They all proposed a unified, orderly universe, governed by one superordinate, logical force.

Yet even this formulation begs the key question, which is, why does our species insist on having religious beliefs at all? Why do we set ourselves up to accept beliefs, to live by theory, either a theory of our own, one we are given, or one we buy into? Why do we reflexively insist on believing in an order?

Before I attempt an answer, let me put to rest the ideas of those readers who think they are spared this challenge because they are convinced they have an Aristotelian grasp on matters and currently do not possess any of the off-the-shelf beliefs available to the world culture. You believe current beliefs are unsubstantiated acts of faith or worse, ignorance, and that they all belong on the junk heap of human thought. Your belief may classify as a rational belief as opposed to a magical belief, but a belief it is!

I have argued that our propensity to hold religious beliefs comes directly and reflexively from our brain's special capacity to make inference, as well as its special capacity to accept magical thinking. Further, since at some point the system cannot continue to endlessly make new inferences about the structure of the world, it has to place a bet on one. And the minute it does this, data about the possible fallacy of the assumptions implicit in the belief of choice are ignored. More conservatively, the threshold for considering new information goes up because of the natural unpleasantness associated with not believing. It is unpleasant because without a belief in some kind of order there is a sensation of capriciousness, of instability, of lack of control. Our species must have a belief. It guides, it controls, it dictates the rules of behavior. We all demonstrably develop one about ourselves. It is a short jump to imagine how we must also have one about extrapersonal events as well. Call it Christ, Muhammad, or quantum mechanics, these are all beliefs that allow for human action.

Certainly a major challenge to modern man may be to figure out how to transcend current religious beliefs and to move forward into a system that creates interpersonal understanding instead of indifference, even hate. To achieve that, the most difficult obstacle would be to reassure our species on the not-of-this-world, magical level about the part about God and His will and what He thinks about man and about what man should do if he is to please God. Each religion has its own story here, its own start-up account. This magical part is what most religious people would die for, not only to keep it intact but also to promulgate the belief.

Perhaps the hope for quickest change comes from the substantive level. Religion, overall, gives a fairly good prescription for social living. Love thy neighbor, share, be kind, do not lust after friends' worldly goods, and so on. All religions more or less subscribe to these views, and in order to run a society all of these ideas are very helpful and positive. Indeed, it is the reasonableness of these more general substantive points that makes people initially willing to consider the magical part. Then, through the process of valuation I have been talking about, the magical aspect of the belief takes on greater and greater importance. If believers could come to realize there isn't ten cents worth of difference in their substantive plans, perhaps they might then begin to see the magical part for what it is.

CHAPTER 12

After Hours

STUDENTS always ask disquieting questions about relevance. When they are exposed to a new view of a subject, the better among them immediately ask, "What does it mean?" One might expect the sage professor to be the source for this question. The sage professor, however, has learned the payoff for skepticism. He knows that little is actually ever explained in life. The kind of new data that people claim should put one into a state of disequilibrium aren't worth considering. We explain what we *can* explain, not what we want to explain. As a result most things die of their own weight. That is as it should be.

At the same time it is the wonderfully hopeful questioning of each new generation that energizes. After a talk on science, students ask, "So what does brain science have to say about our culture?" I say things like, "Not much." They say that won't do. I ask why not. Every brain scientist in the history of the world who talks about the meaning of neuroscience for larger questions has come off as foolish. They say seventeen studios turned down *E.T.* Maybe your story will take. I say let's go have a drink and we usually talk into the wee hours. Several students have actually interviewed me, and it usually goes something like this.

STUDENT (S.): What are your views on how brain science relates to social process?

M.S.G.: That is a dangerous game. The fact that I have run some experiments in my life does not automatically qualify me to comment on social process from a psychobiologic perspective. Physicists never sound sillier than when they are talking about biology, let alone about social issues. It is most presumptuous.

By and large I think basic scientists should stick to their labs. Our game is scientific method, and trying to fit life's events into a totally rational formula is risky. Let everyone have his or her own pet social idea. Most social ideas are so far from purely rational they have their own life and nothing I say can directly bear on these issues. They exist at another level of organization, a level that transcends current scientific analysis.

S.: So your idea is to stay in the lab and leave the meaty questions of our existence to the likes of Ronald Reagan and Mario Cuomo. You think politics is the art of the possible and all that kind of thing. It is nothing but a patchwork of special interests. I bet you believe that in practice it borders on being atheoretical. It is certainly not the kind of topic scientists would want to dirty their hands with. Well, we know you really don't think that, so let's get on.

M.S.G.: Yeah, but saying that makes my friends a lot more tolerant of my sketches of some social processes. I'll talk about the nexus of science and politics if we can start with a problem. Why should a professor make more money than a janitor? No matter what the culture, such economic distinctions exist, even though they go against many cultural tenets. It is a tough issue. Consider the problem. Jones, a very good janitor, is doing his best at his job. He is working at his full potential, the job just matching his biologic and cultural talents. He also possesses the qualities of decency, honesty, and responsibility—traits that are frequently hard to come by in any group. Jones makes $11,000 per year plus benefits.

On his way to work every morning, Smith the physicist takes note of Jones's existence by greeting him. Smith has a built-in social reason to appear eccentric—he is truly "smart."

In fact, Smith is a hard-working nuclear physicist. He, too, is working at his biological and cultural capacity. Smith makes $52,000 a year. What is the rationale for this discrepancy in salary between two professions?

S.: Do you think the brain sciences are going to be able to answer a question like this?

M.S.G.: I think if the brain scientists can't answer this question at some point in the evolution of their knowledge, then the brain scientists are not only ignoring the major phenomena of our culture, but they are also working in a moral vacuum. But let's take the matter further and observe a most remarkable thing about Jones and Smith. If you measure the amount of time each week they spend working, eating, sleeping, loving, commuting, watching TV, playing with the children, and so on, you will probably find there is not much difference between them. It is also the case that Jones and Smith both like steak, ice cream, wine, Jack Daniel's, vacations, speedboats, tape recorders, bikes, private property, Holiday Inns, and the innumerable other material commodities available in our culture. Why shouldn't our society be set up so that all can have equal access to all of these things? After all, it is not Jones's fault he fails to understand Kepler's laws.

S.: There are a million possible explanations for such realities. Many people would look for economic explanations, others genetic. Why raise such a question? Each culture can cook up a dozen reasons why things work out the way they do.

M.S.G.: The purpose of the exercise is not to seek answers that describe the actual existence of such practices in a culture. I don't want to consider everyday explanations that deal with obvious current economic realities like the properties of supply and demand of specially trained people. Such factors play a role but don't bear on the question I am asking. What first has to be understood is the psychological reality of why egalitarianism never seems to work. The question probes that reality, and I want to know whether a culture could exist that would allow for such equality. None does, but could one? And what would one have to believe about us humans to make it work? Even in a society that could provide equal goods for Jones and Smith, would Smith stand for an equal distribution? If that were true, it seems to me there would be a strong case for moving toward a society that aspired to such goals. One way or the other it is worth knowing the answer, which already is manifestly known. The question is why do members of our species behave this way?

S.: But there are societies that do distribute goods according to need, and far more equitably. That is certainly true of the Communist nations.

M.S.G.: Oh really? Let's look at the Soviet Union. The Soviets purportedly believe in equal distribution. They do not have a world of abundance, but they have enough of everything so that everyone can share equally in the stores of the society. Yet, I know they don't. I was there and I saw at firsthand a Jones and a Smith, and I experienced the differences between theory and practice.

Comrade Smith was a party member, which immediately put him among the chosen. He could travel, which meant he was trusted, and he could tell you ad nauseum about the virtues of a Marxist society. Smith was a charmer, a lovable sort, the sort who reminds one of a Midwest farmer. Russians are the only Europeans who look, act, and talk like Americans, a circumstance that is very disconcerting. With them, one has no sense of cultural inferiority, as one has when talking to the French. These are knee-slapping folks who will belt down a vodka, regale you with stories, and feed you unbelievably bad food till the early hours of the morning. They prefer, however, after their vodka to sip French cognac, and they usually have it. That is, Smith has it. In fact, meat, milk, shoes, and other necessities are readily available to Smith but not to Jones. Jones has to take his commodities where he can find them. In Moscow one sees millions of Joneses walking around with large empty briefcases. Jones can't be sure when a commodity might become available—a meat store might actually have meat, a shoe store, shoes. If, on his way home, he should come across this happy event, he will line up in freezing cold weather in order to obtain a commodity that is always readily available to Smith. He hopes he can go home with a briefcase containing some hamburger. Relative to Smith, Jones has nothing.

Smith is consumed by the need for an even better life. I unknowingly became part of an intricate plot to acquire certain goods for him. After the event had occurred, I smiled and said to him, "Oh, I guess you really don't believe in this equality business, just as William Sloane Coffin doesn't really believe in God?" That was at two o'clock in the morning after much cognac and many laughs. His eyes narrowed and he said, "You must remember, I am a Soviet citizen." Then his eyes glazed over and moments later the party was over. The story is not new. In fact, I can't think of a single person I know who after visiting Russia doesn't tell the same story.

S.: So you think the need to individuate within a social group exists regardless of the social beliefs of a culture.

M.S.G.: It happens at each end of the economic and social scales. Look at affluent communities. Society has distributed vast wealth to each of the folks who live in such places. The community when looked at in this light is a socialist's dream. The question is, what is life like under such unreal circumstances?

All reports come back that our species is up to its old tricks. Family A is trying to outdo family B in car ownership. Nonutilitarian acquisitions abound, and seemingly mindless social superiority is sought in virtually every social and material dimension. In short, in this land of plenty, members of our species are desperately trying to differentiate themselves from their neighbors. The folks agonize over the decisions that allow for independence of expression, of establishing differences among themselves and others. The thought of being in the same boat as a neighbor is not acceptable. Look at things at the other end of the scale.

Consider the !Kung who eke out their living in the Kalahari desert. Anthropologist Richard Lee has written about this small society and makes many remarkable observations. Here, in what is equal but subsistence living compared to the affluent suburb, the !Kung men sit around the campfire and complain about certain members of the community who are not rowing their oar, are not being polite, are not showing humility. In short, the ad hominem remarks are setting a context for differentiating one !Kung from another. The thought of all being the same, having the same, and living the same is as alien to the !Kung as it is to all other members of our species.

And so it goes all over the world. Our species has properties of mind that are common to all its members, and while they are expressed differently from one culture to another, this difference in expression does not undercut the fact that the *Homo sapiens sapiens* brain has certain algorithms for action. It is my belief that failure to honor this reality raises havoc with the personal and societal psychology of our lives.

S.: So you're saying that one behavior that is sort of universal across all human cultures and social systems is that we all seek to differentiate ourselves from others, which frequently leads to acquisitive behaviors that spell the end for egalitarian ideas. I won't argue that the simplest way to achieve differentiation is to acquire more or different goods. But one could accept or reject your thesis without having to refer to brain organization to do so. Why bring in brain science?

M.S.G.: You are quite right that these claims about universality of the species could be simply asserted as a fact of the species and left at that. But that is not the game the scientist likes to play. The aspiration is always to find which claims are actually true and valid for all; and if one finds such a fact, then we all must adjust to its reality. Social theorists can argue ad infinitum.

The natural scientist wants to know what the facts of our species are that will allow us to begin to choose among all the alternatives for social theory, and I think brain science is learning more about our real nature than most disciplines. Then again, I am a partisan to that view. Besides, you are the one who wanted to talk about how brain science might relate to social process.

S.: Okay. Why do you think the way the human brain is organized leads our species to seek differentiation, that is, independent identity?

M.S.G.: It has to do with the left brain's interpreter, which is always busy sorting out the behaviors produced from our many brain modules. The left brain is constantly and reflexively generating theories to explain the internal and external events that occur around us. And it is because of that structure that we always attribute causes to everything that happens to us.

Now it turns out that most of us think things are not going our way as often as they should, and we like to find external causes for our dissatisfaction. As I have said, if a green person walks into my space and I am a blue person, I have found someone to blame. This is the mechanism by which most of our silly prejudices form, but it is part of life and it is always at work. I have heard it argued that the minute Israel obtains a lasting peace with the Arabs, the state will self-destruct because the natural prejudices that now exist among all of the various social groups within Israel will be unleashed. There has never been a heterogeneous culture in the history of the world that has lived at peace.

At any rate I think this same mechanism is at work in simple one-to-one relationships. Mr. X tends to think Mr. Y is the source of his failure to be completely fulfilled. Since living well is the best revenge, Mr. X strives to acquire things Mr. Y doesn't have. His actions may in turn stimulate these same processes in Mr. Y, and the situation continues to spiral. What Mr. X and Mr. Y aspire to is influenced by intrinsic aesthetic sensibilities and intellectual considerations, along with the ever-present effects of environment.

So why should the janitor be paid differently from the physicist? To my way of thinking there is no a priori reason why he should, it just always works out that way; and the reason, no matter what the theory of the overlying social structure and no matter what period in history we speak of, can be traced to these brain principles.

S.: All right, let's talk about these principles specifically. You talk about left brains and right brains. You talk about free will and how its illusory presence is important for the development of human beliefs, which in turn makes us unique and differentiated from the animal kingdom. How can this be pulled together? What does it mean? What is the point of knowing about it?

M.S.G.: Before commenting on that, I want to make sure you understand why I think it is important to recognize the need for individuation. I maintain that such needs represent what might be called "impenetrable characteristics of the species." Nothing in the culture seems to dilute or neutralize the force of these needs, and as a result they should be recognized and accepted.

S.: That is a strong claim, and I want to go over how you arrived at it.

M.S.G.: Okay. It has been commonplace to think that our conscious cognitive self is organized and exists in such a way that our language system is always in complete touch with all of our thoughts. It knows where in our brains to find all the information we have stored there, and it assists in all computations or problem-solving activities we engage in. Indeed, the strong subjective sense we all possess of ourselves is that we are a single, unified, conscious agent controlling life's events with a singular, integrated purpose.

S.: That's what we have been taught, more or less.

M.S.G.: And it is not true. Brain studies show that our cognitive system is organized in modular fashion. That means there are a vast number of relatively independent systems in the brain that compute data from the outside world. These independent systems can deliver the results of those computations to the conscious verbal system, or they can express their reactions by actually controlling the body and effecting real behaviors. In the human brain there is a special capacity, a special system found in the left brain, that interprets the diverse behaviors of these modules and through these interpretations forms beliefs. The left brain is constantly constructing theories about the casual relations among elementary events that transpire inside and outside our heads. These interpretations are reflexively carried out by the left brain because it and only it has the capacity to make inference.

S.: Are you saying animals don't have the capacity to interpret their behavior? A dog can quickly learn not to go into a neighbor's yard.

M.S.G.: Look, it is necessary to distinguish between learned associations and the capacity to make abstract inference. All kinds of animals can do the former—none but the human can do the latter. Making an inference means going beyond the data given and grasping relations among elements.

I hope I made it clear that this inference-making capacity which is the source system for the left-brain interpreter is a system that exists independent of the language system per se. Language reports on its activities, but it is not language qua language doing the job. Another point for the modular brain.

S.: How does the modular brain with its special left-brain systems for inference making relate to any ideas you might have about social attitudes? Can you get there from here?

M.S.G.: I think so. When friends and colleagues are confronted with the question as to what it is they believe to be true about the species that finds them for or against a social issue, they are forced to admit that they do not have crisp theories about human nature; in fact, most of us get along day by day without carrying around an articulated theory. Yet we think we believe in something about human nature that makes us take a passionate stand for or against a social issue.

What are these theories that determine our stands on particular social decisions? And, do the brain and behavioral sciences support one particular view over another? Let's say social program X is proposed and the electorate is called upon to vote on it in a referendum. What is it we think we know about the nature of humans such that we are either for or against such a program?

There are two major implicit beliefs about how humans best respond to social challenge. The primary belief of our culture is what I call the "externalist" view. It is the view that in order to handle the multiple problems of this life—problems deemed so complex it is thought they go beyond any individual's ability to cope—society should set up structures, agencies, institutions to help manage the individual's affairs. Things and people can be fixed by the external administration of circumstances and goods. According to this view, humans are supposed to respond to these externally delivered aids in a very positive way. This view makes certain assumptions about human nature, and therein certain assumptions about brain organization, that I will address.

The other position is what I call the "internalist" view. This view recognizes that personal beliefs are the proper guides for personal action and that by placing responsibility on the person, social groups function better. A key idea is that responsibility for action is an individual responsibility, not the responsibility of any social system. Structuring social systems that remove the centrality of the person, self-perceived as acting freely, becomes the destructive impulse of an externally oriented culture.

Internalists tend to be against an aggregate, social response to a personal problem. They tend to think that in the long run humans are better equipped to deal with the stresses and strains of everyday life on an individual level, and that to construct social support systems that absorb the individual's sense of personal responsibility and transfer it to external institutions is unhealthy for the species. A simple example: instead of having street cleaners, people should have the internalized value that littering the streets is bad behavior. Moreover, internalists tend to believe that once the street cleaner is hired, the mechanism by which human values such as cleanliness are inculcated is seriously undermined.

Clearly the externalist/internalist dichotomy does not begin to tell the whole story or capture all of the subtleties of tacit human beliefs for approving or disapproving of social actions. Yet it does serve as a more or less accurate portrayal of the assumptions about human nature most of us tend to make before deciding on a social position.

S.: Can you tell me more? How does an externalist function?

M.S.G.: Sure. Jane and Bob are disruptive in school. An externalist solution: send them to a counselor. A woman is harassed; go to a women's center. Dairy farmers are not making the profits they deem fitting with their investment; go to the dairy association to lobby for special considerations. Harry can't find work. He is a teacher and the only available jobs are for delivery men. Harry is not enamored with the concept of downward mobility; go to the unemployment office. In our current culture there is an agency, a service group, or an emotional support system for every conceivable problem. At one level it would seem to be a handsome index of our culture's humanity, of its caring. Some might view it as a measure of our culture's guilt response to the overall affluence that abounds, still others as an expression of a special interest group.

I will forgo consideration of these more psychodynamic and sociological views, since, if I considered them, in a very short time I would find myself in a quagmire of hypotheses, each dependent on the rank assumptions of another. Let me simply assert that civilized people of all persuasions naturally want to help the disadvantaged, which is why these societal mechanisms are usually set up. I have no doubt that proponents of both externalized and internalized views are equally charitable. The question is how to achieve the goal without violating the psychological and biological principles of the species. In the present context let me identify the psychological assumptions that underlie the notion that (a) offering an external support system is a good idea, and (b) such a system is organic with respect to how the human is naturally built.

The major psychological assumption present in the externalist view is that the organism is primarily responsive to the contingencies of externally offered rewards and, moreover, that most human behavior can be explained by contemplating an individual's environmental contingencies. An environment can be structured with an intricate set of rewards strategically placed throughout its landscape such that all eventualities can be positively dealt with and order maintained. That is the behaviorist idea as commonly stated, and a vast number of our current social programs are constructed in this spirit. The externalist devalues the concepts of personal responsibility and is ready to let responsibility be a function of institutional systems. The externalist sees the concept of personal responsibility as an illusionary construct with no real meaning or value. In this reductive view, humans are irrevocably connected to the actual physical environment. Since it is the environment that metes out rewards and punishments to individuals, it is well, if not preferable, for the social structure, not the individual, to be the responsible entity. Remember our discussion about intrinsic motivation?

Externally motivated rewards are not effective at controlling behavior. Something in the human conscious agency intervenes and guides behavior. It is something that is interesting, this "stuff," these mental properties of the human mind, and it is these properties we are trying to learn more about. My point is not that the powerful effects of reward on behavior do not have interesting implications for understanding behavior, but that they are limited in scope. They deal neither with the interesting dimensions of human consciousness nor with the major discoveries made in the brain and psychological sciences over the past two decades.

S.: So what does an internalist do?

M.S.G.: Susan loses her parking ticket after parking for only one hour. She believes you pay for your mistakes, so she does not seek special consideration. She pays for a full day. Bill loses his job; he finds another one and develops new skills. Grandmother becomes senile; the children take her in. A graduate student wants a thesis project outlined; Mike tells him to find another advisor. This is the posture of people with the internalist view of matters. One reacts to life's problems by calling upon the internalized values of a lifetime that emphasize beliefs in personal management and personal responsibility as far as possible. A key notion is that when people are held accountable for their own decisions and actions, they become singularly capable of responding to environmental surprises.

But when the accountability function is tacitly or explicitly assumed by a societal institution, people begin to adopt antisocial behaviors whereby the concept of personal responsibility becomes perverted, and general social welfare is in fact derailed. Instead of viewing life in a contributory way, life's game becomes a scheme that is tied closely to increasing personal consumption. It happens to corporate executives and it happens to the ghetto poor. Overregulation results in the antisocial response of self-aggrandizement.

The internalist believes that as individuals are relieved of responsibility for personal management, the strong perception that each of us has of being freely acting organisms becomes fixated, by necessity, only on the accumulation of things and services for personal well-being no matter what the implications for societal cost. The internalist believes that externalist programs produce results that are precisely the opposite of those intended.

The internalist believes our species should capitalize on the emancipating attribute of humans, the capacity to make inferences that go beyond the immediate relations perceived, and through this hypothesis-generating system form beliefs. And since beliefs are formed by actual behaviors, the management of cultural rewards is profoundly important for the workings of a healthy society. This view can be generalized to suggest that societies are better organized and more workable when there is least central organization to them. Societies work better when identifiable people are held personally responsible for their actions.

The major assumption in the internalist view is that those personal beliefs perceived as being freely arrived at allow for the formation of internal principles, which in turn influence a person's particular responses to external reward and punishment. There is, then, what might be called a superordinate construct present in the human mind that is free to override a human's response to environmental contingencies.

The research I have reported demonstrates that specific brain areas in the left hemisphere of most humans generate hypotheses concerning the separate actions a person engages in as the result of either external or internal contingencies. These personally generated hypotheses about our own behavior receive a special status and can in turn modulate or facilitate future behavioral responses.

According to my model, the brain is constructed in a modular fashion in which particular modules would be free to respond to the literalness of environmental contingencies. Yet a brain system built in a modular way would also need a single interpreter to explain the various behaviors emitted over time by the modules, enabling a human to construct a unified theory of self, an activity most of us have carried out. It turns out the brain is organized in precisely such a fashion.

S.: Since all humans possess human brains why doesn't the interpreter module click in and overrule the interest in rewards and punishments for all of us as it seems to do for internalists? I know what your view of the internalist is. These are people who sort of take advantage of their special human brain features and let the beliefs that naturally form in all of us become an internal guide for action. They try not to engage in human activities merely as a function of external reward or avoid them for fear of punishment. The transcendent beliefs established by the left brain's interpreter guide behavior, right?

M.S.G.: We are getting closer. My point is, of course, that all humans when closely scrutinized do behave alike. Beliefs established by the left brain's interpreter bringing order to our behaviors are as richly present in the externalist as they are in the internalist. Needless to say, these processes are also active in people heavily dependent on externalist social programs. That is why structuring an artificial, make-do environment that elicits dependent behaviors is so dangerous. The interpreter module is going to have to make sense out of such a strange world, and beliefs about the nature of things emerging in such an environment are going to become quite odd. Ever heard of welfare rights, that is, the right to receive welfare?

It is frequently said that most social programs are a disaster. The existence of programs that deal only with symptoms causes strange behaviors to occur that become perversely powerful in changing certain personally held, socially necessary beliefs. Beliefs such as personal accountability, cooperative behavior, personal generosity, trust, and a host of others become perverted.

Why externalists fail to see that I don't know. Why they insist on continually proposing external programs with their unarguable antisocial implications for transferring responsibility for action from the individual to society is another matter. It has to do with latent or not-so-latent elitism. But let's not get into that.

S.: Most practicing externalists know nothing of these concerns. And the ones that do say the personal cost to the individual is worth the price of having solved the original problem. Quite simply, the externalist sees a social problem and wants to help solve it. It is the "We are rich and don't want to feel guilty about it, so let's throw money and bureaucrats at the problem" attitude. I can live with that mainly because I never am clear what the internalist would do when it is clear something must be done.

M.S.G.: You want to get practical, even though what I am arguing for is a realignment of a conceptual view of humans such that future policymakers become sensitive to the real nature of our nature. I want to halt the reflex toward externalism that besets us all. But I know you want to be concrete. Well then, let me take it from the top.

In my most expansive moment I would argue that brain and behavioral sciences have gained knowledge about the mechanisms responsible for our brain's unique propensity to form beliefs and to evaluate them. A consequence of this process for humans is that we are free, by having beliefs, to override responses to immediate gains and losses offered up by the environment. This feature of the human brain dooms the species to be endlessly inventive and resistant to environmental regulation. The more regulated its environment, the more the species withdraws from responsible participation in the social structure and becomes wholly interested in self-gain.

This same species' specific ability to form beliefs allows for the appearance of certain behaviors essentially unique to the species, behaviors like considering the future, planning the present, and others that transcend the need to live on the thin edge of today. Yet these vastly important dimensions of human culture have occurred with positive value only when humans function in a society regulated as loosely as possible, and where individuals are perceived as being personally responsible for their actions. When humans function in a highly regulated social context, the unique human capacity becomes self-oriented and fixates on personal well-being. The ever-present human perception of "self-willed" action, of what the human is responsible for, narrows and falls to new levels of parochialism.

I am arguing, therefore, a most counterintuitive point. I am claiming that a culture becomes more caring and humane the more its citizens feel themselves to be part of the problems that beset their lives. The only sure way to bring them close to such problems is to structure a culture where they deal with the problems at a personal level.

S.: This is a general view. How does this translate to specifics?

M.S.G.: There is not one among us who would not like to lead a problem-free life. My first reaction to letting a social institution deal with a problem is one of assent. After new social institutions resolve a few problems, I expect them to continue to do so. Suddenly the administration begins to slow down. Other programs they started are costing much more than anticipated and are not functioning efficiently. People are taking advantage of them. People don't treat an institution as a personal friend, and no one seems able to find the source of this view because all inquiries produce the same answer: the problem is elsewhere. The culture has developed institutions that have their own lives and continue independently of the problems they were formed to address. But the culture must yield to the demanding public that now expects all problems to be solved by external agencies, and instead of correcting what is basically uncorrectable, more attempts are made by borrowing more money and setting up more agencies that won't work. This downward spiral is the oldest story in the world. It is sort of an uncontestable reality that has beset every age of human history.

The issues handled by these schema are usually ones of social and ethical justice, such as care for the "needy." These issues rankle, and a dispassionate analysis is usually impossible.

Everyone wants to appear caring and, in the egotistical competition to prove themselves humane, people never deal with the underlying issues. In order to avoid the usual chest poundings, let me analyze a biomedical problem that has a direct impact on the life of the average citizen. It deals with our culture's planned response to the increasing social problem of senile dementia. It is a problem that is not going to go away. If we could cope with this kind of social issue, we would begin to better cope with the others.

Modern medicine's brilliant advances have created a bizarre state of affairs by prolonging life without preventing brain disease. Senile dementia afflicts approximately 16 percent of people over the age of sixty-five. This problem was nonexistent when life expectancy was lower. Now as modern medicine raises life expectancy with every new somatic cure, the absolute number of elderly people with healthy bodies goes up. Senile dementia is already so ubiquitous that virtually all of us are familiar with the disease.

The reason externalists are making proposals for the management of senile dementia is that the senile person can be a disruptive social entity. A once-sentient grandparent, once capable of regaling all with stories of life, now can't speak coherently. Sequential behavior becomes impossible.

The socially oriented externalists combine their interests with those of the business-oriented externalists and argue in favor of building nursing homes, old age homes, and other baby-sitting institutions. A personal family responsibility is assumed by the state or by a private institution. The disturbing stimulus is removed from the family, usually to the relief of the relatives, and the paramedical businessman is delighted with new and expanding profits from the upkeep payments of either the private or public sector.

This short-term externalist solution works only with a small number of people. By 1990 it is estimated that it will cost society over thirty-five billion dollars a year to care for this population in America alone. That kind of price tag is not allowable; the culture cannot support it. There is, in short, no workable externalist solution, and the advent of a scientific solution is not even close.

The internalist solution requires a lot of discipline, but it works. The demented person has to be cared for through much smaller units and, for the most part, such care will have to be an obligation of the family. Instead of baby-sitting cooperatives, there will be senile-sitting cooperatives. The middle-class, comfortable family will have to appreciate that this responsibility is a personal one and not call for a social solution.

S.: One last thing, what have you got against religion?

M.S.G.: Nothing, why?

S.: Implicit in your theory about how beliefs are formed is that all beliefs are relative. That means that you do not believe in one true faith.

M.S.G.: I am trying to help elucidate the mechanisms of belief formation and I hope we are coming to a better understanding of how these mechanisms work. Religious belief is a nice example of how the process works. Religious scholars, by and large, chart the historic course of particular religions, and the more brilliant among them try to unearth conflicts in religious dogma not only existing among faiths but also within faiths. They then try to look at how outside social and historic forces act upon those belief systems. My interest is quite different. I want to get at the question of why people possess such beliefs in the first place. Why do humans develop and maintain such magical beliefs?

S.: That explains your interest in the early beliefs of the Egyptians and Mesopotamians and the distinctive difference in their beliefs being related to environmental variables. But a more general point is that ever since the Enlightenment, the educated mind has drifted away from actually believing in organized religion. Scientific beliefs as well as an accurate knowledge of historical process seem to have taken the place of religious belief. Do you really think any educated person believes in revealed truths anymore? Early humans had no choice.

M.S.G.: I hear you but I don't buy it. Bill Buckley believes. Donald MacKay believes. Sir John Eccles believes. Even Dave Premack is heavy on mysticism. No one can accuse that crowd of being short on worldliness. They all have word processors, medications in their bathroom cabinets, investments in Comsat and gene splicing—and yet they still possess rather simple faiths. And certainly if you did a likability analysis, there are just as many lovely people in this world who believe as who don't. That any particular belief can be dissected and its contradictions illuminated with relatively little ease is completely beside the point. We are a believing species. And we believe both because of the way our brains are organized and because of certain capacities we have, in the left brain.

S.: Your argument, then, as to why we humans form beliefs is as follows. The brain is organized in terms of independent processing modules and each can generate behaviors. These behaviors, which can be either internally executed or externally monitored, are then interpreted by special nonlanguage processes usually present in the left half-brain. "The Interpreter" module, call it TI, then reports on its hypothesis about the causal relation among things to the left-brain language centers, which we will call TT for "the talker."

M.S.G.: That's pretty much it.

S.: And because we humans more or less automatically make hypotheses about our elicited behaviors that are freely generated, a sense of our generated beliefs or thoughts as being freely willed is extremely strong. Related to this reality is the fact that when externally imposed laws or customs are forced upon us with no choices possible for alternative responses, TI is not engaged in a way that forces us to alter our personal beliefs. It is given an easy out by virtue of the fact that no decision is being personally made that requires a personal interpretation and therefore attributes the reasons for action as simply due to the external system that created the imposition.

M.S.G.: Yes, but there is another point. I am saying that because we now know our brains are organized in this fashion, certain social organizations are doomed. In particular I am saying the externalist (who is privately an internalist since he too possesses a human brain with a TI) who argues for curing social ills with reward schemas is harming the species because he is setting up an artificial environment for certain people that those people must interpret. And sadly, the down-and-out recipient can't write off the externally imposed rewards and simply accept the fortuitous goods. Such a recipient in Western societies is usually free to choose alternatives. Because of that his TI is clicked in and has to explain why the fortuitous goods are being accepted. That's the psychological moment when the antisocial hypotheses start and when the social systems begin to crack. The externalist, then, is setting up societal landscapes that are destructive.

S.: From what you say I really wonder whether or not there is any hope that our species can learn to live together when various groups maintain and wish to impose different beliefs about the nature of things. Since there is no changing the brain property that insists on this belief feature of human activity, the only hope is that humans will grow to appreciate how beliefs are formed and, by knowing that, begin to realize, at least to some extent, their relative nature.

M.S.G.: I don't know. I can remember standing in the old Jewish section of Jerusalem, looking down at the Wailing Wall, then looking up above it at the magnificent mosque Al-Aqsa, and then smelling the incense wafting over from the Church of the Holy Sepulcher. There in Israel millions of people have guns pointed at one another because of the beliefs about the value of that small piece of real estate. Arabs and Jews alike are ready to lie, to cheat, to kill either to protect or to conquer in order to call that piece of earth their own. On the surface the human situation is very real and beliefs about the importance of the issue have filled newspapers and books for nearly forty years. And to fully appreciate the problem, one has to be clear about the subjective intensity one experiences when holding a belief.

There was a time in my life when receiving absolution followed by receiving Holy Communion gave rise to the most intense feelings of worth imaginable. I was raised according to a set of rules for living, rules that brought order and speed to my decisions about how to behave, and I had lived by them, with a few minor infractions, for a long time. Communion was the celebration of this contract, and it was a very sweet experience. That submission to the rewards such beliefs can offer is, of course, what keeps millions of people subscribing to them.

Clearly there is no budging the Arab, the Jew, or the Christian from his or her similar pleasures of mind and heart. With all of the archaeological, biological, psychological, and historical data in the world pointing out how beliefs are formed, the true believers quietly say they understand all of this, but that the inquisitor does not understand a fundamental issue. They, as opposed to the others, are correct!

We all know this and respect it, but I know something too. I know that everybody has an effect on everybody else. I hope that my book has spelled out some of the organic reasons why our species generates and maintains beliefs of all kinds. With that knowledge, perhaps all of those who possess beliefs at odds with the beliefs of others will, upon quiet consideration, become more tolerant.

NOTES

Chapter 2

1. Roger W. Sperry, "The Growth of Nerve Circuits," *Scientific American* 201 (1959): 68–75.

2. John B. Watson, *Behaviorism* (New York: Norton, 1925).

3. Paul Weiss, "Nerve Patterns: The Mechanisms of Nerve Growth," *Third Growth Symposium* 5 (1941): 163–203.

4. Roger W. Sperry, "Mechanisms of Neural Maturation," in S. S. Stevens, ed., *Handbook of Experimental Psychology* (New York: Wiley, 1951), 236–80.

5. Roger W. Sperry, "Chemoaffinity in the Orderly Growth of Nerve Fiber Patterns of Connections," *Proceedings of the National Academy of Science* 50 (1963): 703–10.

6. Paul H. Patterson and Dale Purves, *Readings in Developmental Neurobiology* (Cold Spring Harbor, N.Y.: Cold Spring Harbor Laboratory, 1982).

7. David H. Hubel and Torsten N. Wiesel, "Receptive Fields, Binocular Interaction and Functional Architecture in the Cat's Visual Cortex," *Journal of Physiology* 165 (1962): 559–68; and David H. Hubel and Torsten N. Wiesel, "The Period of Susceptibility to the Physiological Effects of Unilateral Eye Closure in Kittens," *Journal of Physiology* 206 (1970): 419–36.

8. Fernando Nottebohm, "Ontogeny of Bird Song," *Science* 167 (1970): 950–56; and Fernando Nottebohm, "Brain Pathways for Vocal Learning in Birds: A Review of the First Ten Years," *Progress in Psychobiological and Physiological Psychology* 9 (1980): 85–124.

9. Joseph Altman, "Postnatal Growth and Differentiation of the Mammalian Brain with Implications for a Morphological Theory of Memory," in Gardner Quarton, Theodore Melnechik, and Francis O. Schmidt, eds., *The Neurosciences: A Study Program* (New York: Rockefeller University Press, 1967), 723–43.

10. Paul I. Yakovlev and Andre R. LeCours, "The Myelogenetic Cycles of Regional Maturation of the Brain," in Alexandre Minkowski, ed., *Regional Development of the Brain in Early Life* (Oxford: Blackwell, 1967).

11. Mark R. Rosenzweig and Edward L. Bennett, eds., *Neural Mechanisms and Memory* (Cambridge, Mass.: M.I.T. Press, 1976).

12. Giorgio M. Innocenti, "The Development of Interhemispheric Connections," *Trends in Neurosciences* 4 (1981): 142–44.

13. Bryan T. Woods, "The Restricted Efforts of Right Hemisphere Lesions After Age One: Wechsler Test Data," *Neuropsychologia* 18 (1980): 65–70.

14. Alf Brodal, *Neurological Anatomy,* 2d ed. (New York: Oxford University Press, 1969).

15. Richard L. Sidman and Pasko Rakic, "Neuronal Migration with Special Reference to Developing Human Brain: A Review," *Brain Research* 62 (1973): 1–35.

16. Mark A. Berkley, "Vision: The Geniculo Cortical System," in R. Bruce Masterson, ed., *Handbook of Behavioral Neurobiology: Sensory Integration* (New York: Plenum Press, 1978).

17. Jack R. Cooper, Floyd K. Bloom, and Robert H. Roth, *The Biochemical Basis of Neuropharmacology* (New York: Oxford University Press, 1978).

18. Floyd K. Bloom; D. Segal; N. Ling; and R. Grillemin, "Endorphins: Profound Behavioral Effects in Rats Suggest New Etiological Factors in Mental Illness," *Science* 194 (1976): 630.

Chapter 3

1. Ronald E. Myers and Roger W. Sperry, "Interocular Transfer of a Visual Form Discrimination Habit in Cats After Section of the Optic Chiasm and Corpus Callosum," *Anatomical Record* 115 (1953): 351–52; and Roger W. Sperry, "The Corpus Callosum and Interhemispheric Transfer in the Monkey," *Anatomical Record* 131 (1958): 297.

2. Roger W. Sperry, "Cerebral Organization and Behavior," *Science* 133 (1961): 1749–57.

3. Andrew J. Akelaitis, "Studies on Corpus Callosum: Higher Visual Functions in Each Homonymous Field Following Complete Section of Corpus Callosum," *Archives of Neurology and Psychiatry* (Chicago) 45 (1941): 788; Andrew J. Akelaitis, "Studies on Corpus Callosum: Study of Language Functions (Tactile and Visual, Lexia and Graphia) Unilaterally Following Section of Corpus Callosum," *Journal of Neuropathology and Experimental Neurology* 2 (1943): 226; Andrew J. Akelaitis, "Study of Gnosis, Praxis, and Language Following Section of Corpus Callosum and Anterior Commissure," *Journal of Neurosurgery* 1 (1944): 94; and Andrew J. Akelaitis et al., "Studies on Corpus Callosum: Contribution of Dyspraxia and Apraxia of Corpus Callosum," *Archives of Neurology and Psychiatry* (Chicago) 47 (1942): 971.

4. Joseph E. Bogen and Peter J. Vogel, "Cerebral Commissurotomy in Man: Preliminary Case Report," *Bulletin of the Los Angeles Neurological Society* 27 (1962): 169; and Michael S. Gazzaniga, Joseph E. Bogen, and Roger W. Sperry, "Some Functional Effects of Sectioning the Cerebral Commissures in Man," *Proclamation of the National Academy of Science USA* 48 (1962): 1765–69.

5. Roger W. Sperry, "Brain Bisection and Mechanisms of Consciousness," in Sir John C. Eccles, ed., *Brain Mechanisms and Conscious Experience* (New York: Springer-Verlag, 1965); and Michael S. Gazzaniga and Roger W. Sperry, "Language After Section of the Cerebral Commissures," *Brain* 90 (1967): 131–48.

Chapter 4

1. Robert E. Ornstein, *The Psychology of Consciousness* (San Francisco, Calif.: Freeman, 1972).

2. Michael S. Gazzaniga, Joseph E. Bogen, and Roger W. Sperry, "Some Functional Effects of Sectioning the Cerebral Commissures in Man," *Proceedings*

of the National Academy of Sciences USA 48 (1962): 1765–69.

3. Joseph E. Bogen and Michael S. Gazzaniga, "Cerebral Commissurotomy in Man: Minor Hemisphere Dominance for Certain Visuospatial Functions," *Journal of Neurosurgery* 23 (1965): 394–99.

4. Jerre Levy, "Psychological Implications of Bilateral Asymmetry," in Stuart J. Dimond and J. Graham Beaumont, eds., *Hemisphere Function in the Human Brain* (New York: Halsted Press, 1974).

5. Jerre Levy, Colwyn Trevarthen, and Roger W. Sperry, "Perception of Bilateral Chimeric Figures Following Hemispheric Deconnection," *Brain* 95 (1972): 61–78.

6. Michael S. Gazzaniga and Joseph E. LeDoux, *The Integrated Mind* (New York: Plenum, 1978).

7. Michael S. Gazzaniga, Joseph E. Bogen, and Roger W. Sperry, "Observations of Visual Perception After Disconnection of the Cerebral Hemispheres in Man," *Brain* 88 (1965): 221.

8. Joseph E. LeDoux, Donald H. Wilson, and Michael S. Gazzaniga, "Block Design Performance Following Callosal Sectioning: Observations on Functional Recovery," *Archives of Neurology* 35 (1978): 506–8.

9. Robin Yin, "Looking at Upside-down Faces," *Journal of Experimental Psychology* 18 (1969): 141–47.

10. Michael S. Gazzaniga and Charlotte S. Smylie, "Facial Recognition and Brain Asymmetries: Clues to Underlying Mechanisms," *Annals of Neurology* 13 (1983): 536–40.

11. Robert Nebes, "Perception of Spatial Relationships by the Right and Left Hemispheres of Commissurotomized Man," *Neuropsychologia* 11 (1973): 285–89.

12. Brenda Milner and Laughlin Taylor, "Right Hemisphere Superiority in Tactile Pattern Recognition After Cerebral Commissurotomy: Evidence for Nonverbal Memory," *Neuropsychologia* 10 (1972): 1–15.

Chapter 5

1. Michael S. Gazzaniga, Donald H. Wilson, and Joseph E. LeDoux, "Language, Praxis, and the Right Hemisphere: Clues to Some Mechanisms of Consciousness," *Neurology* 27 (1977): 1144–47.

2. J. J. Sidtis; B. T. Volpe; D. H. Wilson; M. Rayport; and M. S. Gazzaniga, "Variability in Right Hemisphere Language Function After Callosal Section: Evidence for a Continuum of Generative Capacity," *The Journal of Neuroscience* 1 (1981): 323–31; and M. S. Gazzaniga; C. S. Smylie; K. Baynes; W. Hirst; and C. McCleary, "Profiles of Right Hemisphere Language and Speech Following Brain Bisection," *Brain and Language* 22 (1984): 206–20.

3. John J. Sidtis; B. T. Volpe; J. D. Holtzman; D. H. Wilson; and M. S. Gazzaniga, "Cognitive Interaction After Staged Callosal Section: Evidence for Transfer of Semantic Activation," *Science* 212 (1981): 344–46.

4. Michael S. Gazzaniga and Joseph E. LeDoux, *The Integrated Mind* (New York: Plenum Press, 1978).

5. Joseph E. LeDoux, Donald H. Wilson, and Michael S. Gazzaniga, "A

Divided Mind: Observations on the Conscious Properties of the Separated Hemispheres," *Annals of Neurology* 2 (1977): 417–21.

6. Michael S. Gazzaniga and Charlotte S. Smylie, "What Does Language Do for a Right Hemisphere?" in Michael S. Gazzaniga, ed., *Handbook of Cognitive Neuroscience* (New York: Plenum Press, 1984).

7. Michael S. Gazzaniga, "On Dividing the Self: Speculations from Brain Research," in W. A. den Hartog Jager et al., eds., *Proceedings of the 11th World Congress of Neurology* (Amsterdam: Excerpta Medica, 1978); and Michael S. Gazzaniga and Bruce T. Volpe, "Split-brain Studies: Implications for Psychiatry," in Silvano Arieti and H. Keith H. Brodie, eds., *American Handbook of Psychiatry*, vol. 7, *Advances and New Directions* (New York: Basic Books, 1981).

8. Leon Festinger, *A Theory of Cognitive Dissonance* (Stanford, Calif.: Stanford University Press, 1957).

Chapter 6

1. Juin A. Wada and Theodore Rasmussen, "Intracarotid Injection of Sodium Amytal for the Lateralization of Cerebral Dominance: Experimental and Clinical Observations," *Journal of Neurosurgery* 17 (1962): 266–82.

2. Gail Risse and Michael S. Gazzaniga, "Well-kept Secrets of the Right Hemisphere: A Carotic Amytal Study of Restricted Memory Transfer," *Neurology* 28 (1976): 950–93.

3. Bruce T. Volpe, Joseph E. LeDoux, and Michael S. Gazzaniga, "Information Processing of Visual Stimuli in an Extinguished Field," *Nature* 282 (1979): 722.

4. Robert Ruff and Bruce T. Volpe, "Reduplication of the Local Environment After Right Parietal and Right Frontal Brain Injury," *Journal of Neurology, Neurosurgery, and Psychiatry* 44 (1981): 382–86.

5. M. S. Gazzaniga; J. E. LeDoux; C. S. Smylie; and B. T. Volpe, "Plasticity in Speech Organization Following Commissurotomy," *Brain* 102 (1979): 805–15.

6. Michael S. Gazzaniga, "Right Hemisphere Language Following Brain Bisection: A 20-year Perspective," *American Psychologist* 38, no. 5 (1983): 525–37.

7. M. S. Gazzaniga; C. S. Smylie; K. Baynes; W. Hirst; and C. McCleary, "Profiles of Right Hemisphere Language and Speech Following Brain Bisection," *Brain and Language* 22 (1984): 206–20.

8. Jean Piaget, *The Child's Conception of the World* (New York: Harcourt, Brace, 1929).

9. David Premack, *Intelligence in Ape and Man* (Hillsdale, N.J.: Erlbaum, 1976).

Chapter 7

1. Michael S. Gazzaniga, "The Biology of Memory," in Mark R. Rosenzweig and Edward L. Bennett, eds., *Neural Mechanisms of Learning and Memory* (Cambridge, Mass.: M.I.T. Press, 1976).

2. William B. Scoville and Brenda Milner, "Loss of Recent Memory After

Bilateral Hippocampal Lesions," *Journal of Neurology, Neurosurgery, and Psychiatry* 20 (1957): 11–21.

3. Brenda Milner, "Les Troubles de la mémoire accompaynant des lesions hippocampiques bilaterales," in P. Passaurant, ed., *Physiologie de l'hippocampus* (Paris: Centre Nationale de la Recherche Scientifique, 1962).

4. Larry R. Squire and Robert Y. Moore, "Dorsal Thalamic Lesions in a Noted Case of Chronic Memory Dysfunction," *Annals of Neurology* 6 (1979): 503–6.

5. Neal J. Cohen and Larry R. Squire, "Preserved Learning and Retention of Pattern Analyzing Skill in Amnesia: Dissociation of Knowing How and Knowing That," *Science* 210 (1980): 207–9.

6. Neal J. Cohen and Larry R. Squire, "The Amnesic Patient H.M.: Learning and Retention of a Cognitive Skill," *Society for Neuroscience Abstracts* 7 (1981): 235.

7. Elizabeth R. Warrington and Larry Weiskrantz, "The Amnesic Syndrome: Consolidation or Retrieval?" *Nature* 228 (1970): 628–30.

8. William Hirst and Bruce T. Volpe, "Temporal Order Judgments with Amnesia," *Brain and Cognition* 1 (1982): 294–306.

9. Kathleen Redington, Bruce T. Volpe, and Michael S. Gazzaniga, "Failure of Preference Formation in Amnesics," *Neurology* 34 (1984): 536–38.

10. B. T. Volpe; P. Herscovitch; M. E. Raichle; M. S. Gazzaniga; W. Hirst; and D. C. Derrington, "PET Defined Metabolic Abnormalities in Transient and Chronic Amnesia," *Neurology* (in press).

11. Jeffrey D. Holtzman and Michael S. Gazzaniga, "Dual Task Interactions Due Exclusively to Limits in Processing Resources," *Science* 218 (1982): 1325–27.

Chapter 8

1. Anthony Marcel, "Conscious and Unconscious Perception: An Approach to the Relations Between Phenomenal Experience and Perceptual Processes," *Cognitive Psychology* 15 (1983): 238–300.

2. Michael S. Gazzaniga, Jeffrey D. Holtzman, and Charlotte S. Smylie, "Speech Performance Without Cognition" (in preparation).

3. John Campion, Richard Latto, and Y. M. Smith, "Is Blindsight an Effect of Scattered Light, Spared Cortex, and Near-threshold Vision?" *The Behavioral and Brain Sciences* 6 (1983): 423–86.

4. Jeffrey D. Holtzman, Bruce T. Volpe, and Michael S. Gazzaniga, "Deficits in Visual/Motor Control Despite Intact Subcortical Visual Areas," *Neurology* 34 (suppl.) (1984): 187; and Jeffrey D. Holtzman, "Interactions Between Cortical and Subcortical Visual Areas: Evidence from Human Commissurotomy Patients," *Vision Research* 24 (1984): 801–13.

5. J. J. Sidtis; B. T. Volpe; J. D. Holtzman; D. A. Wilson; and M. S. Gazzaniga, "Cognitive Interaction After Staged Callosal Section: Evidence for a Transfer of Semantic Activation," *Science* 212 (1981): 344–46.

6. M. S. Gazzaniga; J. D. Holtzman; J. Gates; M. D. F. Deck; and B. C. P. Lee, "NMR Verification of Surgical Section of the Human Corpus Callosum and Presence of the Anterior Commissure," *Neurology* (in press).

7. Michael S. Gazzaniga and Charlotte S. Smylie, "What Does Language Do for a Right Hemisphere," in Michael S. Gazzaniga, ed., *Handbook of Cognitive Neuroscience* (New York: Plenum Press, 1984).
8. Stephen Kosslyn, *Image and Mind* (Cambridge, Mass.: Harvard University Press, 1981).
9. S. Kosslyn; J. D. Holtzman; M. Farah; and M. S. Gazzaniga, "A Comprehensive Analysis of Mental Imagery Generation: Evidence from Functional Dissociations in Split-brain Patients," *Journal of Experimental Psychology: General* (in press).

Chapter 9

1. Judson Mills, "Changes in Moral Attitudes Following Temptation," *Journal of Personality* 26 (1958): 517–21.
2. Leon Festinger and J. Merrill Carlsmith, "Cognitive Consequence of Forced Compliance," *Journal of Abnormal and Social Psychology* 58 (1959): 203–10.
3. Arthur R. Cohen, "An Experiment on Small Rewards for Discrepant Compliance and Attitude Change," in Jack W. Brehm and Arthur R. Cohen, eds., *Explorations in Cognitive Dissonance* (New York: Wiley, 1962).
4. M. Ross, "Salience of Rewards and Intrinsic Motivation," *Journal of Personality and Social Psychology* 32 (1975): 245–54.
5. Donald M. MacKay, *Freedom of Action in a Mechanistic Universe: The Eddington Lecture* (Cambridge, U.K.: Cambridge University Press, 1967).

Chapter 10

1. Gary Lynch, personal communication.
2. Jacques Tixier, personal communication.
3. Leon Festinger, *The Human Legacy* (New York: Columbia University Press, 1983).
4. Edward O. Wilson, *Sociobiology* (Cambridge, Mass.: Harvard University Press, 1975).
5. Richard Nisbett and Lee Ross, *Human Inference: Strategies and Shortcomings of Social Judgment* (Englewood Cliffs, N.J.: Prentice-Hall, 1980).
6. Yves Coppens, *Exposé sur le cerveau: Le cerveau des hommes fossiles* (Paris: Institut de France, Académie des Sciences, 1981).
7. Michael S. Gazzaniga and Charlotte S. Smylie, "Facial Recognition and Brain Asymmetries: Clues to Underlying Mechanisms," *Annals of Neurology* 13 (1983): 536–40.
8. Ofer Bar-Yosef, "Prehistory of the Levant," *Annual Review of Anthropology* 9 (1980): 101–33.
9. Robert J. Wenke, *Patterns in Prehistory* (New York: Oxford University Press, 1980).
10. David Premack, "Reinforcement Theory," in David Levine, ed., *Nebraska Symposium on Motivation* (Lincoln, Neb.: University of Nebraska Press, 1965).
11. Henri Frankfort; H. Frankfort; J. A. Wilson; T. Jacobsen; and W. A.

Irwin, *The Intellectual Adventure of Ancient Man* (Chicago and London: The University of Chicago Press, 1946, 1977).

Chapter 11

1. Norman Geschwind, "Behavioral Change in Temporal Epilepsy," *Archives of Neurology* 34 (1977): 453; Norman Geschwind, "Editorial: Behavioural Changes in Temporal Lobe Epilepsy," *Psychological Medicine* 9 (1979): 217–19; and Norman Geschwind, "Interictal Behavioral Changes in Epilepsy," *Epilepsia* 24, suppl. 1 (1983): S23–30; Norman Geschwind, "Pathogenesis of Behavior Change in Temporal Lobe Epilepsy," in Arthur A. Ward, Jr., J. Kiffin Penry, and Dominick P. Purpura, eds., *Epilepsy* (New York: Raven Press, 1983).

2. Stephen G. Waxman and Norman Geschwind, "Hypergraphia in Temporal Lobe Epilepsy," *Neurology* 24 (1974): 629–36.

3. Patricia Phillips, *The Prehistory of Europe* (Bloomington, Ind.: Indiana University Press, 1980).

4. Robert J. Wenke, *Patterns in Prehistory* (New York: Oxford University Press, 1980).

5. John A. Wilson, "Egypt," in Henri Frankfort; J. A. Wilson; T. Jacobsen; and W. A. Irwin, *The Intellectual Adventure of Ancient Man* (Chicago and London: The University of Chicago Press, 1946, 1977).

6. Ibid.

7. George Boas, *The History of Ideas* (New York: Scribner's, 1969).

8. Ibid.

INDEX

Index

Index